SpringerBriefs in Psychology

Behavioral Criminology

Series editor

Vincent B. Van Hasselt, Fort Lauderdale, USA

More information about this series at http://www.springer.com/series/10850

David L. Shapiro · Angela M. Noe

Risk Assessment

Origins, Evolution, and Implications for Practice

Springer

David L. Shapiro
Center for Psychological Studies
Nova Southeastern University
Fort Lauderdale, FL
USA

Angela M. Noe
Center for Psychological Studies
Nova Southeastern University
Fort Lauderdale, FL
USA

ISSN 2192-8363 ISSN 2192-8371 (electronic)
SpringerBriefs in Psychology
ISSN 2194-1866 ISSN 2194-1874 (electronic)
SpringerBriefs in Behavioral Criminology
ISBN 978-3-319-17057-2 ISBN 978-3-319-17058-9 (eBook)
DOI 10.1007/978-3-319-17058-9

Library of Congress Control Number: 2015935408

Springer Cham Heidelberg New York Dordrecht London

Printed on acid-free paper

Springer International Publishing AG Switzerland is part of Springer Science+Business Media (www.springer.com)

Contents

Introduction

I learned that murderers die for their crimes
Even if we make a mistake some time

(Tom Paxton, 1962)

Tom Paxton was not a psychologist, nor was he involved in doing risk assessments of the potential for future violence. Nevertheless, these two lines from a song he wrote in 1962—entitled "What did you learn in school today?"—highlights some of the concerns we will be raising in this volume: The "mistake," in this case, pertains to the accuracy of the conclusions we derive when we perform an assessment to determine the risk for future violence. For example, of the 32 states in which the death penalty is permitted, 26 of them allow information to be presented to the jury about an individual's potential for future violence. This information (regarded as an aggravating circumstance) is provided during the sentencing phase, in which the jury is tasked with determining whether the appropriate sentence for the crime is death or life in prison. As we shall see, the research in this area is limited in terms of the ability to predict violent behavior; yet, this question—"Doctor, will this man be dangerous?"—is frequently asked of mental health professionals who serve as expert witnesses in capital cases. Despite the paucity of available research to back up the validity of such forecasts, many have no compunction about rendering their opinions.

There are many areas of the law in which predictions of the potential for violence play a significant role. For example, United States v. Salerno (1986) discussed the issue of the potential for violence with regard to decisions made during bail hearings. Further, decisions regarding probation/parole conditions often entail a concern for whether the person will pose a danger to others. Since the landmark case of Lessard v. Schmidt (1972), the process of civil commitment has been based on the concept of "danger to self or others" by reason of mental illness.

The range of the areas mentioned above, in which the prediction of violent behavior carried great weight, assumed or presupposed that clinicians were able to make such assessments with a high degree of accuracy. In fact, the early terminology involved the "prediction of dangerousness," a dichotomous kind of opinion. In other words, the mental health professional decided if the person was dangerous or not dangerous; there was no "middle-ground." Indeed, prior to critical analyses of the research and additional studies highlighting the flaws of these judgments, there was an untested assumption that mental health professionals had clinical abilities that could ferret out "dangerousness" during an extended clinical interview. There was, however, little attention directed to what clinicians assessed during their evaluations, nor the methods utilized. Further, such assessments were highly idiosyncratic in that most clinicians did not follow any sort of standardized protocol for their evaluations, which made it difficult for researchers to evaluate the accuracy of the prediction methodology used.

During the 1960s, the case of Baxstrom v. Herold (1966), in the state of New York, revealed some groundbreaking news about the risk of violent behavior posed by psychiatric patients. In this case, a class action suit was filed on behalf of psychiatric inpatients at the Dannemora State Hospital in New York. The court ordered 966 of these patients released or transferred to less secure facilities. There were dire predictions made by a number of people regarding the fact that there would be a great deal of violent acting out based on previous clinical assessment of these individuals. Yet, as it turned out, very few of the cohort from Baxstrom acted out. Steadman and Cocozza (1974) found that only 20 % had been reconvicted, predominantly for nonviolent offenses. This served as the beginning of a new era, in which the unquestioned assumption that mental health clinicians could predict future violence would be challenged. For example, Steadman and Cocozza (1976) reported that the assumption that clinicians had the ability to predict future violent behavior had little scientific basis.

During the late 1970s and into the early 1980s, Monahan started to review the research. Interestingly, as of the late 1970s, there were only five research studies on the accuracy of clinicians predicting violent behavior. Monahan (1981) reported an unsettling discovery: In our predictions of future violent behavior, we were essentially wrong two out of three times. That is, based on clinical assessments alone (which, at that time, consisted primarily of clinical interviews), psychiatrists and psychologists were accurate no more than one out of every three predictions made concerning violent behavior. These findings were based on results obtained over several years with institutional populations that had both committed violence in the past (and, thus, had high base rates for it) and who were diagnosed as mentally ill (Monahan 1981, p. 47). This was a rather dramatic finding that challenged the foundation upon which much of our clinical work was based.

Monahan further noted in his work that the best predictors of violent behavior among the mentally ill were, in fact, the same predictive factors found in populations that were not mentally ill. Of these factors, he concluded that the strongest was a history of past violence. The poorest predictors were those valued by clinicians, which included diagnosis and personality structure. He was also critical of mental health professionals for ignoring base rates in their research. To clarify, a base rate is the percentage that identifies the occurrence of a particular behavior in a certain group. For instance, the base rate of violent behavior in the general population is about 2 %. That is, 2 out of 100 individuals—on average—will act in a violent manner. Ultimately, the assessment of the prevalence of violent behavior among mentally ill patients is only meaningful when compared to the base rate found in the general population.

Although questions were being raised regarding the accuracy of these predictions of future violent behavior, the judicial system moved on as if these issues were not troubling. Whether this was due to the fact that researchers did not want to raise the issues in court, or they were raised and the courts ignored them, is a matter or some speculation that is beyond the scope of this volume. Suffice it to say, several major court decisions seemed to ignore the concerns that psychological research was raising regarding the prediction of violent behavior.

In Jurek v. Texas (1976), for instance, the Supreme Court reviewed the three statutory aggravating factors for Capital cases in Texas. The first involved the individual's probability of committing criminal acts of violence that would constitute a continuing threat to society. If the State proved, beyond reasonable doubt, that all three were present, the sentence was death. If any of the three were not applicable, then the sentence would be life imprisonment. The other two factors were whether the conduct was deliberate with a reasonable expectation that death would result, and that the conduct was an unreasonable response to any provocation. The appellants in Jurek argued that the factor about future violence was "unconstitutionally vague" and, therefore, lacked merit. The Supreme Court rejected this argument, stating that future dangerousness is commonly addressed and answered throughout the American Criminal Justice System and, further, that it is no different from any other prediction of future behavior. They went on to cite the relevance of this factor in many other legal decisions, such as bail, sentencing, and parole. The court noted that such prediction may be difficult, but it is not impossible.

The issue about prediction of future violence was again raised in a subsequent case, namely Estelle v. Smith (1981). However, the issue was addressed in a peripheral way, dealing with the inadequacy of the examining psychiatrist's methodology: Predicting future violent behavior based on a diagnosis. Based on a brief clinical interview, the psychiatrist in question, Dr. James Grigson, concluded that Smith showed no remorse and, therefore, he was a sociopath. He further elaborated that since sociopaths, by definition, commit criminal acts, Smith would be violent in the future. As distressing as this inadequate examination and conclusion is, it should be kept in mind that is not what the United States Supreme Court is concerned with. Rather, the Supreme Court addresses matters in which there may be a violation of the constitution; therefore, the court would only address issues about inadequate assessment if it is directly linked to a constitutional violation.

In Smith's case, the court was focused on possible violations of the fifth and sixth amendments to the constitution. The fifth amendment deals with the fact that one need not incriminate oneself in their statements, and the sixth amendment deals with having legal representation at a "critical stage of the proceedings." Smith was not told that Dr. Grigson would be testifying for the State in Smith's sentencing hearing, and was led to believe that he was being interviewed as part of a competency evaluation. Smith's statements, later taken out of context and used to establish the fact that he was a sociopath (and, therefore, dangerous), essentially amounted to self-incrimination. Generally, a competency evaluation was not seen as a critical stage of the proceedings; however, an evaluation to determine whether he would be violent and, consequently, eligible for the death penalty would be a critical stage of the proceedings and would require the availability and assistance of counsel. Ultimately, the court found that Mr. Smith's being led to believe that the interview was only a competency evaluation was a violation of both his fifth and sixth amendment rights. Smith's case was reversed and remanded, with Smith eventually sentenced to life in prison rather than to death.

The final case in which the court essentially dismissed the concerns raised by mental health professionals was Barefoot v. Estelle (1983). In this case, the same Dr. Grigson, along with a Dr. Holbrook, testified for the State. Not surprisingly, their response to hypothetical questions reflected an opinion that Thomas Barefoot would probably commit further acts of violence and, thus, would represent a continuing threat to society.

Psychiatrists and psychologists both recognize that the rendering of an opinion about an individual without having examined him or her is professionally unethical. Nevertheless, Dr. Grigson testified that he was 100 % certain and absolute that Barefoot would kill again, even though he had never even examined him. Barefoot's attorneys argued that the use of psychiatric testimony at a sentencing hearing about future violent behavior was unconstitutional, as such professionals are not competent to predict future violent behavior. Given that their predictions were likely to result in erroneous judgments, it was argued that their usage constituted violations of his eighth amendment (cruel and unusual punishment) and fourteenth amendment (equal protection under the law) rights. Ultimately, the court rejected all of the petitioner's arguments. The Supreme Court affirmed the conviction and the sentence.

The court handed down a number of opinions in response to the case of Barefoot v. Estelle. For example, it was noted that not letting psychiatrists testify about future dangerousness would be equivalent to "disinventing the wheel." They cited the case of Jurek v. Texas as affirming the fact that this was a legitimate issue to be considered in capital cases and that any methodological deficiencies could be "cured by rigorous cross-examination." The court also chided the Amicus Brief filed by the American Psychiatric Association (which argued for the elimination of such testimony), arguing that there are many psychiatrists who disagree with that position. The certainty with which Dr. Grigson made his predictions was also addressed. More specifically, the court stated that such a declaration of certainty is a matter of weight to be given to the testimony, not to its admissibility. Finally, addressing the issue of hypothetical questions, the court observed that hypotheticals and responses to them are an acceptable part of the judicial process. In essence, once again, the court rejected the concerns of mental health professionals about the true ability (or lack thereof) to predict future violent behavior.

Chapter 1
Origins

The MacArthur Foundation Research on Risk Assessment

As previously mentioned, Monahan set out to look at the reasons for the very poor predictive validity of clinical work. Harking all the way back to the literature from the 1950s, he suggested that perhaps we would be better off doing purely actuarial assessments rather than continue relying on unaided clinical assessments. These clinical assessments were done on an individual basis, using a diagnostic formulation approach. Actuarial assessments, on the other hand, provide results based on a strict algorithmic formula (or "equation"). Stated more simply, these assessments look for the presence of a specific combination of static, fixed, and largely demographic risk factors that have been "weighted," meaning the number of points assigned to each item is based on the purported strength of its relationship with violent behavior. For example, on one specific measure, the Violence Risk Appraisal Guide (VRAG), the endorsement of past violent behavior contributes more points (+6) to the final numerical score than, say, marital status (+1), a personality disorder diagnosis (+3), or history of alcohol problems (+2).

It should be noted that the specific risk factors on actuarial measures require the evaluator to focus on variables that do not change over time and, perhaps more importantly, are able to be studied far more precisely than clinical judgment; however, this approach deliberately ignores individual variations that do not fit the pattern. Returning to the VRAG as an example, the item, "lived with both biological parents until age 16" ("Yes" is assigned a weight of −2 and No is assigned a +3) generalizes the statistics from a specific group of subjects in such a way that the person who did not grow up with both biological parents until age 16 is assumed to be more likely to engage in violent behavior than someone who did live with both parents until age 16. Fundamentally, these instruments ignore individual variations, such as the fact that a divorce may have resulted because of abuse or a separation due to military service. Clearly, these variations simply do not matter when looking at violence from a purely actuarial point of view.

Despite Monahan's skepticism, as well as his statements that actuarial methods were superior to clinical judgment, he nevertheless became the principal

D.L. Shapiro and A.M. Noe, *Risk Assessment*,
SpringerBriefs in Behavioral Criminology, DOI 10.1007/978-3-319-17058-9_1

investigator in the MacArthur Risk Assessment Studies. These studies, which inevitably grew into a rather comprehensive research-based assessment model, incorporated many clinical variables into the actuarial data. The MacArthur model became one of the bases for an approach called "Structured Professional Judgment" (SPJ) or, as it is sometimes called, Structured Clinical Judgment. The MacArthur research primarily involved monitoring psychiatric populations. Further, their approach involved the incorporation of several assumptions for evaluation, such as: The fact that all relevant information is available, that the term "prediction" applies to a specific behavior within a limited time period, and that training could yield high inter-rater reliability.

In time, Monahan discovered three factors that seemed to be limiting the previous research: (1) A constricted range of risk factors—that is, clinicians would try to predict future violent behavior after looking at a few demographic variables, or an impression from a clinical interview, or the results from one psychological test. Thus, they were making rather broad statements based on very little data; (2) Weak criterion measures—Monahan found that most of the studies were using "re-arrest" as the selection variable for inclusion in the study. Clearly, this is a requirement that is far too narrow and restricts the number of individuals who can be included. In other words, the specified definition underestimates the true rate of violent behavior, as such acts often do not lead to an arrest (especially in cases of domestic violence) or, conversely, an alternative intervention may be used (e.g., getting the individual hospitalized). Monahan also found this to be the case with regard to the patient population they were monitoring (i.e., males with a history of previous violence). So, once again, only a narrow segment of that specific population was being considered for participation. Finally, the research was based on findings from a single site, meaning generalizations were made that ignored the possible effects of differences in socio-economic status or cultural background.

To rectify these limitations, the MacArthur research made a conscious decision to improve the study's reliability and validity by: (1) Studying a large and diverse array of risk factors; (2) Expanding the criterion variable of re-arrest to also include patient's self-report and input from a large variety of collateral sources, such as family interviews and hospital records; (3) Including both male and female participants; and (4) Collecting data from multiple sites. It did not take long for the researchers to realize that greater focus needed be placed on risk factors that were relatively robust predictors compared to the previous, albeit limited, findings. Among these were: Psychopathy, difficulties regulating anger, the presence of delusions and/or hallucinations, diagnosis, gender, the endorsement of violent thoughts, abuse as a child, a history of previous violence, and, lastly, a variety of contextual variables. It is important to add that these efforts ultimately led to the replacement of the commonly used presumptuous terminology "prediction of dangerousness" with the term "risk assessment."

Early on in the research, the investigators noticed that a main effects regression model (which is part of the development of the actuarial "equation" described earlier, including the weighting assigned to specific items) did not improve predictive accuracy. Consequently, they opted for a "classification tree model" in lieu of a linear regression model approach. The classification tree model is similar to the regression model, except it involves identifying discrete categories rather than numerical scores—thus, this stage attempted to classify individuals into groups according to their proposed level of risk. It should be clarified that the specific questions asked at any point during the assessment were based on the respondent's answer to the question that preceded it rather than a fixed list of questions to ask all of the participants (which is typically the case for regression model approaches). Basically, it was hypothesized that the specific, empirically-based risk factors that would be important to explore during one individual's risk assessment may, in fact, not be relevant to the risk assessment of another. Truly, this use of a classification tree model represented a major departure from the methodology that was typically used in other studies, as it was more individually tailored and did not rely on a "one size fits all" model; however, they found that the initial predictive accuracy of this decision tree model was not substantially better than the main effects regression model. This, obviously, represented an issue that needed to be addressed before they could move forward.

To deal with the predictive validity issue, the investigators decided to focus on the "extreme" cases, since they could not classify all people as high or low risk. In essence, the average cases falling between the extremes would be considered to be the same as the base rate. Using multiple risk estimates, the researchers noticed that a high risk on many classification trees was correlated with an individual who is more likely to be violent, especially compared to those on fewer classification trees. In short, a risk assessment that examined multiple dimensions and had a greater number of options proved to be more accurate than those with a narrower focus.

Overall, the MacArthur research identified four different parameters that should be used to structure any examination of risk factors. This new perspective included: (1) Demographic features, such as age and gender; (2) Historical factors, including prior mental hospitalization and/or history of violent behavior; (3) Contextual variables, such as the degree of social support an individual has, the extent of disinhibiting influences, the degree of inhibiting influences; and (4) Clinical traits, including a broad array of factors having to do with diagnosis and specific symptoms. This model resulted in the identification of well over one hundred risk factors, which could be combined in different ways using the decision trees. As noted earlier, such an approach would use a broader range of information sources, including not only arrest records, but also hospitalizations and input from self-report and collateral sources. In addition, violence would be more clearly specified in terms of types of violence, targets of violence, location of the violence, and timing of the violence.

Essentially, violent behavior was conceptualized as the product of a complex array of interactions among a number of factors (i.e., demographic, psychological, sociological, biological, and contextual factors). Subsequent to this realization, a research protocol was developed to identify the specific features and interactions the researchers should explore further. While this was helpful for determining which risk factors were, in fact, risk factors, it also proved to be useful for ruling out the risk factors that were simply baseless assumptions. An ideal example of this can be drawn from the demographic category: Race was originally identified as a demographic factor for consideration; however, when socio-economic variables were controlled for, the racial factor proved to be an unremarkable contribution. Based on their findings concerning the demographic factors, the researchers highlighted an elevated risk in males between the ages of 18 and 24, especially those who were members of a lower socio-economic group and poorly educated. It should be clarified that these are purely static variables and, for the most part, do not change very much over time.

The researchers also explored a wide variety of psychological variables in an effort to identify measurable risk factors for future violent behavior. This included an examination of the various diagnostic groupings, the impact of certain kinds of mental illnesses (or, perhaps more importantly, the influence of specific symptoms), and the contributions of substance abuse, to name a few. The diagnostic groupings and mental disorders evaluated were not restricted to the "serious mental illnesses" (e.g., major depressive disorder, bipolar disorder, schizophrenia) but also included the potential influence of personality disorders on violent behavior. Specific focus was given to the traits characteristically seen in narcissistic, histrionic, borderline, and antisocial personality disorders, with quite a bit of focus dedicated to the subset of antisocial individuals known as psychopaths. Indeed, it was around this time that a significant amount of research began to emerge dedicated to exploring the relationship between Hare's (1980, 1985, 1991, 2003) construct of psychopathy and violent behavior. According to Hare, the construct of psychopathy can be broken down into two factors: Factor 1 pertains to the interpersonal/affective deficits characteristic of the prototypical psychopath; Factor 2, on the other hand, involves a general antisocial behavior pattern and chronically unstable lifestyle. This construct will be discussed further in the section addressing the Psychopathy Checklist-Revised (PCL-R).

That there exists an innate link between delusions/hallucinations and inevitable violence is an assumption endorsed by many, especially within the context of the media. For example, it is often presumed that a mentally ill person will eventually act out in response to delusions of persecution or at the behest of auditory hallucinations. Yet, the research evidence substantiating this belief is, at best, mixed. In this specific study, delusions (in general) were not found to be highly correlated with violent behavior; however, a rather powerful association did appear when the experience involved what the investigators deemed "thought control override." Namely, this involved delusions in which the patient felt that another was controlling his/her mind and, as a result, felt powerless to resist the influence of the delusions and/or hallucinations; additionally, they reported that patients also acted out in response to delusions in which they perceived others as trying to harm them. While this was an interesting finding, the results nevertheless revealed an inconsistency: The delusions were most often found in chronically withdrawn patients, the same patients who were also identified less likely to act out.

Another particularly interesting finding elucidated during this study involved the influential power of hallucinations. More specifically, they found that the mere presence of auditory command hallucinations was not enough to prompt violent behavior. Rather, only voices characterized as familiar and benevolent were found to be influential. For example, if the patient heard the familiar voice of a loving family member instructing them to take revenge on someone, the patient would be more likely to act out; however, if the voice was unfamiliar or associated with a hostile individual, such compliance was far less likely. Overall, this portion of the MacArthur studies yielded equivocal results: Although there was a greater likelihood of violence found among such patients, the association was not strong.

Not surprisingly, another variable that was given attention during the MacArthur research was the role of anger in violent behavior. The researchers chose to use the Novaco Anger Scale (1983) to assess for this trait, which is a measure that conceptualizes anger as the interaction of three components: Cognitive, arousal, and behavioral indicators. Indeed, they reported that those with high scores on the Novaco Anger Scales were twice as likely to act violently after discharge than those who did not obtain high scores.

Naturally, the sociological point of view entailed the exploration of a number of environmental variables. Take, for instance, the family's approach to problem solving—Did the family encourage or inhibit expressions of violent behavior as a legitimate means of solving an issue? Similarly, did the individual's peer group typically support or try to prevent him/her from engaging in violent behavior? Indeed, Dr. Reid Meloy (2000) highlighted the role sociological factors, or "popular cultural influences," play in violent behavior and urged clinicians to examine an individual's propensity to use weapons (primarily firearms) carefully. He built on his recommendation by developing the Weapons History Assessment Model (WHAM), which assessed for the person's attraction to firearms, his/her skill using the weapon, the selection of reading materials preferred by the individual, and the nature of his/her affective response to firearms. Lastly, loss of employment and general employment instability were also identified as being correlated with the potential for future violence.

The biological point of view was also seen as quite important, although probably less so than is the case today, given the advancements in neurological imaging. This biological perspective is especially relevant when making distinctions between affective (or reactive) violence and predatory violence. People who have a history of traumatic brain injury (TBI) may become quite irritable, overreact to minor irritations, and respond to such irritations in an explosive and potentially violent manner. Consider, for example, the legendary case of Phineas Gage. Gage was a railroad worker who survived a rock-blasting accident in which a metal rod was driven through his head. Prior to this accident, Gage was regarded as pleasant and amicable; after the accident, however, he was noted as more irritable, more impulsive, and more reactive. Indeed, there are some neuropsychologists—such as Adrian Raine—who have elegantly argued that there is a neurological component underlying a great deal of violent behavior. According to Raine, there may even be abnormalities in the brain structure that facilitates or promotes predatory violence. For example, the size of the amygdala has been found to be smaller in individuals categorized as psychopaths compared to that seen in non-psychopaths (Yang et al. 2009a). This region of the brain is linked with feelings of fear, suggesting that psychopaths experience less fear than others (including fear of consequences and fear of shame/scrutiny). Additionally, individuals with less efficient prefrontal lobe functioning, such as psychopaths (Yang et al. 2009b), often present with compromised judgment and poor ability to appreciate the long-term effects of their decisions. Thus, predatory behavior may be endorsed more often in individuals who do not fear the consequences of their actions, are not concerned with the opinions of others, and are primarily interested in instant gratification.

Finally, the MacArthur studies placed a great deal of emphasis on contextual variables. In other words, they found that violent behavior frequently occurred in a specific setting or under specific circumstances, such as workplace settings, family settings, or after the ingestion of drugs and/or alcohol. Random acts of violence, on the other hand, were found to occur far less often. Truly, just looking at an individual's particular pattern can assist with decisions about intervention efforts, such as whether treatment/management should focus on a specific set of variables or the interaction of multiple variables.

Following the exploration of the identified risk factors, the researchers incorporated an additional statistical procedure—referred to as the Area Under the Curve (AUC)—to evaluate the accuracy of their approach. Briefly, this method, which was initially used by oncologists dealing with radiation, gauges the sensitivity and specificity of whatever measure is being used. Numerically speaking, AUC values can range from 0.50 (completely random, as in a coin toss) to 1.00 (absolute certainty). When dealing with measures designed to determine the risk for future violence, typically AUC values indicate the probability that a recidivist will score higher on the measure than a non-recidivist would.

Returning to the use of AUCs in the MacArthur studies, it was reported that their particular methodology allowed the researchers to place their subjects into one of five risk categories with an AUC of 0.88. Further, they found that the frequency of violence in the community demonstrated by each group spanned from 1 to 76 % during the 20 weeks after discharge (Monahan et al. 2001, p. 127). It is worth adding that only variables that were commonly available in a patient's hospital file or able to be assessed during clinical practice were used. A measure was eventually developed based on this method's success and was named the Classification of Violence Risk (COVR). Fundamentally, this model is quite accurate when compared with other methods; however, it is computationally complex in that it entails exploring 40 variables and their interactions.

In summary, the structure suggested by the MacArthur research involves probabilities concerning specific types of violence occurring within a specific context. This approach, which is in stark contrast with the earlier "predictions of dangerousness," truly provides a far more precise picture of an individual's potential for future violence, in that it qualifies the circumstances under which such behavior is more likely to occur. Again, this represents a major departure from the antiquated, "Yes, s/he will be dangerous" or "No, s/he will not be dangerous" that was once so heavily relied upon.

The Supposed Role of Mental Illness

Although already outlined in the section covering the MacArthur research, stereotypes concerning violence among the mentally ill is, quite frankly, pervasive enough to warrant additional discussion.

There is a widespread public perception that the mentally ill are inherently dangerous. Whenever there is an act of seemingly senseless violence, such as the ever-increasing number of active shooter situations emerging in the United States, the role of mental illness is quickly brought into the picture as an explanatory factor. While this is quite unfortunate, it is not entirely surprising because humans seem to have an innate need to be able to explain violence as something only a select few are capable of. Take, for instance, the old "Lycanthropy" myths of the 1800s. Lycanthropy, or the supernatural ability to turn from a human into a werewolf, was one of the dominating theories for explaining the carnage left behind by a "serial killer" during the Victorian years in England and Europe. Typically, this theory was given credence because no one wanted to believe that it was possible for another human being to be so savage.

To recapitulate the point, the assumption that a violent person must be mentally ill is often grossly inaccurate and, to some degree, offensive. For example, Adam Lanza, the 20-year-old active shooter who murdered his mother and then attacked the Sandy Hook Elementary School in Newtown, Connecticut, was reported to have been diagnosed with Asperger syndrome. Immediately after this diagnosis was made public, hotlines began flooding with calls from anxious parents who were concerned that their children (who were also diagnosed with Asperger syndrome) would soon become violent, too. At face-value, this assumption may seem possible; however, the paucity of data to actually support this hypothetical link between Asperger syndrome and violence suggests that it is, yet again, another baseless assumption meant to explain "unexplainable" behavior.

Of course, there are some cases in which symptoms of mental illness do contribute to the violent behavior. It should be clarified, though, that behavior never occurs in a vacuum and always requires outside influences before it can manifest. Although such influences may vary, an overwhelming amount of stress and/or a recent significant loss is almost invariably present. With that being said, let us look at the case of the Virginia Tech shooting, which is classified as the deadliest shooting by a single gunman in United States' history. The perpetrator here, Seung-Hui Cho, had been recommended for hospitalization earlier. Unfortunately, due to a variety of bureaucratic blunders, Cho was (obviously) not detained. In the case of the Columbine High School "massacre," as it is often regarded, the two perpetrators, Eric Harris and Dylan Klebold, were reportedly depressed and suicidal.

Now, the perpetrators in each of these unfortunate scenarios can be categorized as "active shooters." According to the United States' Department of Homeland Security (DHS) the term active shooter refers to "an individual actively engaged in killing or attempting to kill people in a confined and populated area; in most cases, active shooters use firearms(s) and there is no pattern or method to their selection of victims" (2008, p. 2). Clearly, this definition radiates malevolence and instability; however, it may be a mistake to assume that this destructive behavior is uniquely attributable to a mental illness. In fact, there are actually a number of other psychological factors that are far more robust in terms of their predictive value (e.g., personality disorder features, substance abuse). It is unfortunate that these features are often overshadowed by the focus on diagnosis because they are far more informative.

Take, for instance, the previously described active shooter cases. To this day, it is very often speculated that their behavior had to be the result of a mental illness. While it may be true that a mental illness could have had some influence on their decisions, further analysis reveals some key points that conflict with this "knee-jerk" assumption. For example, the assaults were organized and well-planned. Commonly, those who act out because of a mental illness do so with a certain degree of frenzied impulsivity because, quite often, their compromised focus and concentration limit detailed planning. Further, the motives and thoughts documented by the active shooters in their journals and blogs before the crimes, as well as the behavior endorsed during the attacks, highlights a specific set of shared personality traits that are crucial to consider. For example, most of these perpetrators possessed a high degree of entitlement, which allowed them to feel justified taking the lives of others; the documentation left behind indicated that the perpetrators were eager, rather than fearful, to carry out their plans; they were heavily driven by a need for narcissistic gratification in that they strove to surpass/repeat other cases of mass murder (e.g., Harris and Klebold wanted to "outdo" the Oklahoma City bombing and Adam Lanza reportedly had a large chart that included literally hundreds of cases listed on it hanging on his wall); their behavior obviously reveals difficulty with anger control; and, lastly, they displayed immense callousness with no reservations about the far-reaching impact their behaviors would have on the family members and friends of their victims.

This rather cursory overview of their personalities sheds some light on a psychological risk factor that has a far stronger relationship with violence than mental illness (such a depression and schizophrenia): Psychopathy. In essence, psychopathy can be thought of categorically (a psychopath or not a psychopath) or dimensionally (somewhat psychopathic, quite psychopathic, very psychopathic, etc.). Thus, it is possible that these active shooters were, to a degree, more driven by psychopathic tendencies than the symptoms of a mental illness. Similarly, looking for features of malignant narcissism—a diagnosis relatively circumscribed to the psychodynamic literature—can also be useful as it is basically a less extreme version of psychopathy that is characterized by intense grandiosity, antisocial behavior, a sadistic disposition, and, often, paranoia; malignant narcissists are unique from psychopaths in their ability to actually feel loyalty and concern for others (Gabbard 2005, p. 522). It is worth pointing out that neither psychopathy nor malignant narcissism, alone, could bring about such violent behavior, as it is quite rare for active shooters to be female. Therefore, it can be argued that gender (a demographic variable) may play a moderating role in terms of who acts out in such a way. This would certainly be consistent with the MacArthur research findings in that it entails an interplay of variables.

So far, we have discussed the mistaken impression that all mentally ill individuals will be violent and the fallacy that a violent person must be mentally ill. There is, however, a paradox in the data that suggests some slightly increased risk with certain symptoms. In other words, acting out is possible in all mentally ill individuals, although not equally so.

Up until the mid-1980s, the general consensus within the mental health community was that there was no statistically significant correlation between mental illness and violent behavior. Basically, violence among the mentally ill had about the same base rate as violence in the general population when demographic and other historical factors were controlled for (around 2 %). In an influential article published in the American Psychologist, Monahan (1992) spoke about a conclusion he did not want to reach: After looking at data from several different perspectives (not accounting for the sample of patients or their social/demographic factors), he discovered a relationship between mental illness and violence, suggesting the possibility that mental illness *may* be a predictor of violent behavior. When mental illness was defined as psychosis or a major mood disorder, 13 % of the sample reported acting violently. This, of course, is a notable increase from the 2 % noted above. Yet, Monahan made it a point to emphasize that severe mental illness is rare, and any relationship between it and violence is moderate, at best.

While the findings reported in 1992 may seem solid, there were nevertheless some complex methodological issues in the study's design. Positive symptoms, such as delusions and hallucinations, were found to have a positive correlation with violence, while negative symptoms, such as disorganized speech and emotional blunting, had a negative correlation. The delusions characterized as "thought control override," as discussed before, were twice as likely to result in violent behavior. Needless to say, these are intriguing results, but frequently these symptoms co-occur within the same person. As such, making accurate distinctions between which group is experiencing only positive symptoms and which group is experiencing only negative symptoms is very difficult and any conclusions drawn will have limitations.

Case Example

Mr. G was a 38-year-old African-American male with a history of military service being treated at the Veterans Administration (VA) Hospital for delusions related to what he called a "mind control machine." According to Mr. G, he experienced unbearable pain whenever this machine was aimed at him, pain so severe that it one time resulted in a serious automobile accident. He believed that certain religious groups were behind this conspiracy, but was unsure of their motive. He wrote several letters to local authorities—including the police, the mayor, and various city and state representatives—imploring them to use their power to stop the agony these groups were inflicting. Growing increasingly concerned, Mr. G disclosed the conspiracy and its physiological impact to his therapist, who responded, "Tell me more." Mr. G took the response as affirmation that his therapist was privy to the conspiracy.

Since Mr. G had not gotten any reprieve from his pain or the collusion against him from the legislators on a local level, he decided to contact the President of the United States (who, at the time, was Bill Clinton). He received a formal letter from the White House saying, "Thank you for support of my policies." Mr. G took this letter as proof that President Clinton knew about the conspiracy and would help him fight off the perpetrators who were harming him. He loaded up his car with firearms and many rounds of ammunition, taking care to ensure there was enough for him and the President. He then drove across the country and eventually arrived at the Northwest gate of the White House. When Secret Service agents inquired about his reason for being there, Mr. G proceeded to ramble about the conspiracy and the fact that he was there to pick up the President, who had agreed to join him in the fight. Troubled by Mr. G's response, the Secret Service agents asked to see what was in his trunk. Mr. G opened the trunk, which, of course, was full of firearms and ammunition, and was quickly taken into custody. He was eventually arrested and later found Not Guilty by Reason of Insanity (or NGRI).

As noted earlier, there are both mixed and paradoxical findings concerning violence among those with mental illness. While it is true, for example, that mentally ill patients rarely act out violently, there are some select groups for which there is, in fact, a higher likelihood of such behavior (although not at a statistically significant level). That being the case, it is important to consider other moderating variables that could also influence the outcome, such as race, culture, ethnicity, socioeconomic status, and gender. It is not uncommon for some of these variables to cancel out the effects of others. Admittedly, it is a very complex undertaking and any attempt to establish clear correlations will fail because there is no way to separate out such discrete factors.

Predicting Sexual Re-offending

Many of the above noted observations concerning violence in individuals with mental illness are also relevant to the area of predicting sexual recidivism. The prediction of sexual recidivism is far from a new practice, as it can be traced all the way back to the "Sexual Psychopath Laws" of the 1950s. Basically, these laws allowed individuals who had difficulty controlling their sexual impulses to be indefinitely committed within a psychiatric facility. This alternative to incarceration was based on a belief that proper treatment would help these offenders gain insight as to why they engage in the sexually deviant behavior and, as a result, they would cease to act in that manner. As might be expected, an offender was held until he gained sufficient insight and was no longer felt to be at risk of sexual acting out.

The demise of the sexual psychopath laws can be attributed to two factors. First, the development of insight did not seem to translate into reduced sexual re-offending, suggesting that the treatment was just not effective. The second issue came from those advocating for the civil liberties of the individuals who had been committed involuntarily for an indefinite period of treatment. Unlike fixed prison terms, these individuals could theoretically be hospitalized for the rest of their lives against their will. From a civil liberties perspective, then, attorneys were claiming that such commitment laws were unconstitutional. Ultimately, the sexual psychopath laws disappeared by some time in the 1980s.

The sexual psychopath laws existed for around three decades prior to their elimination, and it did not take long for them to make a comeback. The modern statues, which emerged in the state of Washington in the early 1990s, are referred to as "Sexually Violent Predator" (SVP) laws. Unlike the earlier sexual psychopath laws, which were seen as an alternative to incarceration, the SVP laws allowed for commitment *after* an individual had served his prison term. Usually (but not necessarily), the offender had to have been incarcerated for a sexual offense. Typically, the individual would be referred for an evaluation if, for example, the state raised a concern about the possibility/probability of sexual violence during a parole hearing. This evaluation would determine whether or not the offender "fits" the statutory definition of a sexually violent predator.

The statutory definitions of what constitutes a sexually violent predator are not without issues. While the precise wording differs slightly from state to state, the core requirement is that the individual has to suffer from a mental abnormality or personality disorder which predisposes him to predatory acts of sexual violence. This rather circular definition poses some very real problems for the mental health professional. First, according to the various psychiatric and psychological texts, there is no such thing as a "mental abnormality." This term, which is so broad that it is virtually meaningless, does not actually identify any clear causal relation with sexually violent behavior. Further, there is no existing personality disorder that lists "predatory acts of violence" in its diagnostic criteria. This legal definition is essentially a legislative construct, a fiction, that has nothing to do with what clinicians deal with in their practices. This poses a very real problem for individuals doing such evaluations because they basically have to adopt the language specified in the statute despite its lack of clinical meaning. It is also ethically questionable because we must only reach a conclusion or diagnosis when there is "sufficient data" to justify such a conclusion or diagnosis. How can we find sufficient data to justify a diagnosis that does not exist?

The laws dealing with involuntary commitment across the country speak of the fact that there must be an imminent danger to self or others, usually defined as a recent overt act. Sexual offenders, on the other hand, qualify for what has been called a "special kind of involuntary commitment." In other words, these individuals are not required to have been recently violent in order to be committed. Clearly, this is the case since this population has been incarcerated for a number of years. In other words, with the exception of an exceedingly violent and disruptive prisoner, a recent overt act would not be present. Therefore, the commitment is based exclusively on the ability to "predict future sexual offending."

Also concerning is the fact that these offenders are being committed for treatment; yet, there is no accepted and empirically-validated treatment actually available for them. Many programs do what they *think* would be effective, but there is little or no empirical data to back up the effectiveness of these theoretically-based treatment programs (especially when it comes to long-term risk). As an example, one state contracted with a provider who purported to use a treatment program called "rational self-counseling." There is absolutely no literature that describes rational self-counseling as a treatment, let alone an effective treatment for sexually violent individuals. One might just assume that "the price was right" and the state granted the treatment contract to this group.

In the wake of many of these concerns, several lawsuits came to the attention of the United States Supreme Court. The first was a case entitled *Kansas v. Hendricks* (1997), which involved a man named Leroy Hendricks who was an admitted pedophile. Hendricks was challenging his commitment to an SVP treatment center because it would equate to double jeopardy for he had already served about 15 years in prison for a sexual offense. Given that this assertion represents a violation of the United States Constitution, the case was reviewed by the Supreme Court. The court ended up rejecting his argument because, as they argued, the initial detention was meant to be punishment and the second detention was for the purpose of treatment. In its opinion, the court recognized that there was no effective treatment for this condition, but ultimately explained that this does not equal a total lack of treatment options. It appears the court was committing itself to the purpose of the second commitment rather than the lack of effective treatment, which *is* the basis and justification for their commitment.

In a subsequent case, *Young v. Weston* (1995), the court considered the claims of a committed individual named Andre Young. Young had been sent to a treatment center for sexually violent predators in the state of Washington and asserted that since he was not receiving any treatment, it was technically double jeopardy. The Supreme Court did not deal with this interesting issue, but instead remanded it to the state of Washington for consideration of the adequacy of their treatment programs for sexually violent predators.

Finally, in the case of *Kansas v. Crane* (2002), the court did come close to dealing with a profoundly troubling issue: What exactly was the link between a mental illness and the inability to control sexual impulses? While several other issues were discussed in this case, the court agreed that the involuntary commitment of sexually violent predators could only meet constitutional muster if there was a link between the mental illness and the inability to control the sexual impulses. According to the court, if there was no such link, then the case would be more appropriately handled by the criminal justice system. Truly, if states were to actually follow these suggestions, no one would be committed because the "mental abnormalities" described earlier are, once again, nothing more than legislative constructs.

There is also a profound ethical issue raised by the way these laws are written. For example, the laws allow for the completion of the evaluation and report based solely on a review of records if the individual refuses to cooperate. While this practice is permitted by the law, it is incredibly unethical. Indeed, the Code of Ethics of the American Psychological Association states that one reaches a diagnosis, conclusion, or recommendation only when there are data sufficient to substantiate it, and, except in very rare circumstances, must include a personal interview. If that personal interview cannot be completed, then the report, recommendation, and diagnosis must be qualified in terms of their limited validity and reliability. In the experience of one of the authors (D.S.), it is rare for an examiner to actually qualify his/her conclusions in such a way (beyond the quintessential statement that the defendant would not cooperate, that is).

Chapter 2
Assessment Instruments

We now have a vast amount of data regarding risk assessments from the point of view of demographic, psychological, sociological, biological, and contextual bases. We also have a variety of different techniques to utilize all the way from the straight (unaided) clinical method, the purely actuarial or adjusted actuarial model, and the structured professional judgment approach. We have judgment calls to make in fields as diverse as violence (in general), domestic violence, and sexual violence. We have groups of professionals writing articles proclaiming their instruments to be superior to all others and, further, that all the others do not meet a "standard of care in the assessment of violent behavior." What are we to do with this dizzying array of approaches, and the claims of each to be superior over the others? Or the fact that manipulation of statistics can actually be used to "prove" the superiority of one method over another, meaning there may not be a truly superior instrument to choose?

With the exception of unaided clinical judgment, which most people do not utilize in modern practice, the various approaches to risk assessment are essentially equivalent in their ability to assess violent behavior. After an extensive and exhaustive review of the different risk assessment approaches, Heilbrun (2009) concluded that carefully used, structured professional judgment is just as accurate as actuarial assessment. It is fascinating that people who favor the actuarial approach frequently contrast their findings with those of unaided clinical judgment, not even acknowledging that there is an alternative technique out there called structured professional judgment. This amounts to beating a dead horse, since no one is claiming that unaided clinical judgment still has utility these days.

Another conceptual issue that should be mentioned has to do with placement of the individual into a risk category, or group. Just because a person is assigned to a certain category based on the results of an evaluation does not necessarily mean s/he will fit the entire pattern, as there may be specific idiographic factors that differentiate this individual. This is, essentially, what the adjusted actuarial approach is about; however, those advocating for the purely actuarial model contend that any type of adjustment is merely a throwback to clinical judgment. Those utilizing adjusted actuarial approaches, however, argue that they use the actuarial model

D.L. Shapiro and A.M. Noe, *Risk Assessment*,
SpringerBriefs in Behavioral Criminology, DOI 10.1007/978-3-319-17058-9_2

as an anchoring point and then refine that anchoring point with specific idiographic data. Basically, when we obtain a predictive value for someone in a group, depending on certain other variables, the actual predictive statement may be even higher (or lower). If, for instance, an individual scores in the moderate range on a risk assessment measure but has a mental illness, presents with features of psychopathy and paranoia, has a history of self-medicating with illicit substances, refuses to take his prescribed medication, is unemployed, and has a history of traumatic brain injury, the risk of future violent behavior would more likely be quite high than moderate. Consequently, the importance of modifications to the overall likelihood must be considered.

A final issue worth discussing is that there may not be sufficient data available to make an assessment in any given case. For example, we may not have a complete or factual mental health history, an accurate assessment of the presence of a personality disorder, incomplete records relating to previous violence (or the individual not telling the truth about it), and no records relating to the person's employment status. In the event there is such a scarcity of information, we need to be able to say that there is insufficient data to make a complete assessment.

Let us now look at several risk assessment instruments, both actuarial and those described as structured professional judgment. We will start with the Psychopathy Checklist-Revised (PCL-R) as many of the other tools utilize a PCL-R score as one of their most robust variables.

Psychopathy Checklist-Revised (PCL-R)

The PCL-R can be thought of as an update and combination of the 16 personality traits outlined by Cleckley (1976), who spoke of the psychopath as presenting "a mask of sanity." Robert Hare updated this concept based on his own clinical experience in correctional settings and sought to build on the existing knowledge by developing a system by which to assess for the construct. The resultant Psychopathy Checklist (Hare 1980) has been revised twice since its induction (hence, PCL-R). The first revision of the Psychopathy Checklist (Hare 1991) was limited in its applicability to diverse offender groups. The second edition, described by the author as a "conservative" revision (Hare 2003, p. 1), expanded the standardization data to include a variety of other offenders (e.g., African-American offenders, female offenders, sex offenders, substance abusers, and younger offenders; Hare 2003, p. 2). It is interesting that the PCL-R was not designed with a specific focus on violence risk assessment; yet, its total score is identified as a variable for consideration on many of the available risk assessment instruments.

The PCL-R is composed of 20 items, each of which gauges for an essential behavior pattern or trait inherent in the prototypical psychopath (Rogers and Graves-Oliver 2003). These 20 items are divided into two groups, regarded as Factors, and then each Factor is further subdivided into two Facets. The items in

Factor One assess for the interpersonal (Facet One) and affective (Facet Two) deficits inherent in the construct of psychopathy. Not surprisingly, these variables have been found to be positively correlated with measures of narcissism and negatively correlated with measures of state/trait anxiety (Harpur et al. 1989). The Factor One items include:

(A) Facet One—Interpersonal:

- (a) Glibness, superficial charm;
- (b) Grandiose sense of self-worth;
- (c) Pathological lying; and,
- (d) Conning and manipulative interpersonal style.

(B) Facet Two—Affective:

- (a) Lack of remorse or guilt;
- (b) Shallow affect;
- (c) Callousness and lack of empathy; and,
- (d) Failure to accept responsibility for one's actions.

The items in Factor Two, on the other hand, assess for the lifestyle (Facet Three) and the antisocial (Facet Four) behavior patterns characteristic of the prototypical psychopath. These variables have been found to be positively correlated with measures of sensation-seeking and impulsivity (Harpur et al. 1989). The specific Factor Two items include:

(A) Facet Three—Lifestyle:

- (a) Need for stimulation and proneness to boredom;
- (b) Parasitic lifestyle;
- (c) Lack of realistic long-term goals;
- (d) Impulsivity; and,
- (e) Irresponsibility.

(B) Facet Four—Antisocial:

- (a) Poor behavioral controls;
- (b) Early behavioral problems;
- (c) Juvenile delinquency;
- (d) Revocation of conditional release; and,
- (e) Criminal versatility.

The Factors and Facets that comprise the PCL-R were determined by means of a factor analysis performed to identify the most meaningful combination of the variables possible. There are two additional components not included in the Factors that have been identified as part of the construct of psychopathy, namely Promiscuous Sexual Behavior and Many Short-Term Marital Relationships (Hare 2003).

Indeed, many of the items listed in Factor One and Factor Two correspond fairly closely to the diagnostic criteria for Antisocial Personality Disorder found in the *Diagnostic and Statistical Manual of Mental Disorders, Fourth Edition, Text Revision* (*DSM-IV-TR*) (American Psychiatric Association 2000). Psychopathy is not an official diagnosis in the DSM-IV-TR, though, nor does it appear in the DSM-5 (American Psychiatric Association 2013). Therefore, even if someone meets the cutoff score for psychopathy on the PCL-R, they would still be diagnosed as Antisocial Personality Disorder according to the DSM-IV-TR. Some authors (e.g., Hare et al. 1991; Hare 1996) have argued that a diagnosis of psychopathy and a diagnosis of Antisocial Personality Disorder are, in fact, quite distinct. Approximately 60 % of prison inmates meet the DSM-IV-TR criteria for ASPD, but only 20–25 % of that 60 % (approximately 10–15 % of the prison population) endorsed enough of the risk factors to be classified as a psychopath (Hare 2003). This may explain why the Factor One items are considered the core traits of the prototypical psychopath, as most do not overlap with the DSM-IV-TR diagnosis of Antisocial Personality Disorder.

Scoring the PCL-R is both complex and straightforward. A three-point coding system is used to score each item, with a 0 assigned if the risk factor is not present, a 1 if there is some indication that the risk factor is present but not to the degree needed for a full rating of 2, and a score of 2 given if the risk factor is *definitely* present. Each rating is based on the typical functioning throughout the course of the respondent's life (Hare 2003). In other words, the trait must be a stable feature. The highest possible score for the measure is 40, with 30 assigned as the cutoff score by Hare (2003) for a description of psychopathy. In the event that there is limited information available, up to five items may be omitted without invalidating the total score.

The final scores recorded for the PCL-R include a total score for Factor One, a total score for Factor Two, and an overall total score. One should never base these ratings just on self-report and a substantial amount of collateral information is required to do the ratings (Hare 2003, p. 19). Very often, a semi-structured interview is used to give the evaluator an opportunity to observe whether the offender demonstrates any of the factor items during the interaction, such as glibness and superficial charm, grandiosity, and pathological lying. Therefore, both the semi-structured interview and use of collateral data is recommended for completeness.

The PCL-R total score can be viewed as indicative of the degree to which an individual resembles the prototypical psychopath. The general interpretation of the total score on the PCL-R is quite straightforward: A score of 30 or greater indicates the offender can be classified as a psychopath. This categorical option, however, is discouraged by Hare (2003, p. 31) as it is probably not psychometrically defensible. Indeed, Marcus, John, and Edens (2004) have noted that it may be better to think of psychopathy as a continuum rather than a 'yes' or 'no' category. Therefore, a suggested method is to use ranges (Olmi 2005). It is also useful to consider the range of scores on the four Facets to help clarify what makes a particular psychopath unique from others.

While the categorical option may not be psychometrically defensible, it nevertheless provides insight concerning behaviors to expect in individuals who do, in fact, reach the cutoff mark. For example, a total score of 30 or greater may indicate that the offender is likely to violate the terms of a Conditional Release (Hart et al. 1988). Moreover, a score in the elevated range is strongly associated with poor responsiveness to treatment, indicating that certain interventions are contraindicated. Within the area of interpersonal violence, the confirmation of a psychopathy diagnosis should, ideally, be considered when deciding which interventions are appropriate for a particular individual, as well as which would be contraindicated (Boyle et al. 2008).

There are two alternative versions: the Psychopathy Checklist: Screening Version (PCL:SV) (Hart et al. 1995) and the Psychopathy Checklist: Youth Version (PCL:YV) (Forth et al. 2003). The PCL:SV is a 12 item scale based on a subset of PCL-R items that was created during the MacArthur Risk Assessment studies and is often substituted for the PCL-R to save time. This measure includes more Factor One items than it does Factor Two items. The PCL:YV is helpful for the rapidly growing research concerning the juvenile psychopaths and is distinguished from the PCL-R by its rephrasing of select items to make the respective variables more applicable to juveniles. For instance, the PCL-R item Poor Behavioral Controls appears on the youth version as Poor Anger Control and Revocation of Conditional Release appears as Serious Violation of Conditional Release. The examiner needs to be careful when using this instrument on adolescents, however, because many of the items are common in juvenile behavior (e.g., a need for stimulation, impulsivity, failure to accept responsibility) and may fade over time. Theoretically, this is due to the development of areas of the brain responsible for executive functioning that occurs in the later teen years.

It is important to emphasize that only those appropriately trained should administer this instrument (Hare 1998) as it requires a high degree of sensitivity to ensure that the decision-making style is in line with that used during the tool's standardization.

Violence Risk Appraisal Guide (VRAG)

The VRAG is a series of weighted items meant to determine future risk of violent recidivism in adult males (Quinsey et al. 2006). The early stages of the VRAG's development began with a review of the literature to determine measurable risk factors correlated with violence. After, regression analyses were performed using data from samples of Canadian forensic psychiatric patients to determine which of the identified risk factors were the most strongly predictive of violence (Harris et al. 1993). It should be noted that this was a postdictive, rather than a predictive, study comparing factors that characterized one group as opposed to those which characterized another group (violent versus nonviolent). A book conceptualizing the approach was released in 1998; the second edition was released in 2006.

Overall, Quinsey et al. (1998, 2006) identified 12 variables for consideration during the assessment, namely: (1) Lived with biological parents until the age of 16 (except for death of a parent); (2) Elementary school maladjustment;

(3) History of alcohol problems (each of the following gets one point: Parental alcohol abuse, adult alcohol abuse, alcohol involved in index offense, teenage alcohol problem, alcohol involved in a prior offense); (4) Marital status (married receives a negative weight and unmarried receives a positive weight—that is, more likely to act violently); (5) Criminal history score for nonviolent offenses (22 crimes are listed according to a rating system with the most serious being robbery and arson, going down to less serious crimes such as making threats, breaking and entering, forgery of a check, and disturbing the peace); (6) Failure on prior Conditional Release; (7) Age at index offense; (8) Victim injury (death is scored −2, which is the lowest likelihood because this group would be unlikely to repeat the fatal criminal behavior); (9) Female victim (index offense); (10) Personality disorder (positively weighted); (11) Schizophrenia (negatively weighted); and (12) Psychopathy score. While the authors have recommended that the PCL-R be used for this item, they have also acknowledged that its administration may not always be possible or warranted. To compensate for this potential shortcoming, the authors explored psychopathy as a taxon (Harris et al. 1994) and later incorporated the CATS (Quinsey et al. 1998), which is a brief checklist of eight items designed to measure for traits of psychopathy endorsed by the respondent as a juvenile (e.g., suspensions/expulsions from school, arrested under the age of 16).

Total VRAG scores range from −24 to +38 and correspond to 7- and 10-year probability estimates for violent recidivism (Quinsey et al. 2006). The total score is used in conjunction with the VRAG table to interpret the results. The VRAG table is provided in the instrument's protocol and is broken down into two columns: VRAG score and Category of Risk, which denotes the risk level assigned to the corresponding total score (Quinsey et al. 2006). If an offender's total score falls near the cusp of a risk category, a range may be provided to reflect it (Quinsey et al. 2006).

The authors of the VRAG contend that this particular instrument is far superior to clinical judgment, although they do not define precisely what clinical judgment means. Moreover, they are somewhat inconsistent in their opinion about the role of clinical judgment. After developing the Violence Prediction Scheme, Webster et al. (1994) acknowledged that predictive accuracy may be improved if modest adjustments are made, but *only* if the evaluator has good reason to believe that a particular factor is related to the likelihood of violent recidivism in a respondent (p. 57). Four out of the five Violence Prediction Scheme developers crafted the VRAG shortly after and, in their description, offered a different view: "Actuarial methods are too good and clinical judgment is too poor to risk contaminating the former with the latter" (Quinsey et al. 1998, p. 171). Hart (1998) observed that this is an extreme position and that such exclusive reliance on actuarial methods is not appropriate.

It is important to clarify that actuarial assessments, such as the VRAG, will tell us if an individual belongs to a group likely to commit violence; however, they are not able to distinguish which specific members of the said group will definitely commit violence. Actuarials also do not take into account any rare risk or protective factors. It is quite a different approach from the MacArthur studies which we have described, in which they use actuarial assessment instruments as tools for clinical assessment.

Sex Offender Risk Appraisal Guide (SORAG)

Initially developed as an actuarial measure for determining risk of sexual recidivism (Quinsey et al. 1995), the SORAG has been expanded to measure for the risk of *any* type of violent re-offending in adult male sexual offenders. Violent re-offending, as defined by the developers, refers to both sexual and nonsexual forms of violence that involve physical contact with a victim and (Quinsey et al. 1998, 2006). The instrument was not designed to be used with females or with offenders younger than 18 years of age.

The SORAG is a modification of the VRAG that consists of 14 weighted items, 10 of which were retained from the VRAG. The SORAG's development was also retrospective in its design and utilized data collected from a series of follow-up investigations using samples of sexual offenders referred to a forensic psychiatric facility in Canada (Quinsey et al. 1995). Overall, the risk factors were chosen based on whether or not they provided unique contributions to the prediction of violent recidivism. This includes risk factors such as deviant sexual preferences and history of sexual offenses (Quinsey et al. 2006). The SORAG's method was conceptualized in the same two books as the VRAG.

As was mentioned earlier, the SORAG shares 10 items in common with the VRAG, specifically: (1) Separation from parents before age 16; (2) Elementary school maladjustment; (3) History of alcohol problems; (4) Marital status; (5) Criminal history score for nonviolent offenses prior to the index offense; (9) Failure on prior conditional release; (10) Age at index offense; (11) Meets DSM criteria for any personality disorder; (12) Meets DSM criteria for schizophrenia; and (14a) Psychopathy (PCL-R Score) or (14b) Psychopathy (CATS Score) (Quinsey et al. 2006).

The items for which there is no overlap with the VRAG include: (6) Criminal history for violent offenses; (7) Number of previous convictions for sexual offenses; (8) History of sex offenses only against girls under age 14, including the index offense; and (13) Phallometric test results (Quinsey et al. 2006). The incorporation of phallometric test is useful for detecting the presence of sexual deviancy (Campbell 2007).

For the purposes of coding, a variety of information should be obtained to maximize accuracy. This includes the facts pertaining to the index offense(s), as well as details concerning the offender's conduct and behavior as a youth, family and relationship history, history of criminal activities and antisocial behavior, and psychological diagnoses (Quinsey et al. 2006). While interviewing the offender is not required, useful information could probably be obtained through such interaction (that is, certain behavioral traits may be observed that corroborate outside information). After the requisite information has been gathered, the scoring may commence. Like the VRAG, once again, a coding sheet is provided to score the measure. To begin scoring, the evaluator simply goes through the possible scoring options and selects the response most supported by the available information.

Total SORAG scores range from −25 to +51 and, like the VRAG, they correspond to 7- and 10-year probability estimates for violent recidivism. Further, the total score is also used in conjunction with a conversion table that is provided in the instrument's protocol for interpreting the results. This table is divided into two columns: SORAG score and Category of Risk, which denotes the risk level assigned to the corresponding total score (Quinsey et al. 2006). To determine the risk level, the evaluator simply scrolls down the SORAG table until the offender's total score is located. After the offender's total score has been located, the evaluator then records the risk category designated for the respondent's respective total score. If an offender's total SORAG score falls near the cusp of a risk category, a range may be provided to reflect the elevated risk (Quinsey et al. 2006).

Domestic Violence Risk Appraisal Guide (DVRAG)

The DVRAG is a 14-item actuarial risk assessment tool designed to identify the level of risk posed by male perpetrators of intimate partner violence (IPV) (Hilton et al. 2008). The DVRAG is part of a system that includes the Ontario Domestic Assault Risk Assessment (ODARA) (Hilton et al. 2004), a shorter version of the DVRAG to be used by frontline officers to inform decision-making, such as bail (Hilton et al. 2008). The DVRAG, on the other hand, provides a more comprehensive assessment (Hilton et al. 2010). The DVRAG includes all 13 of the ODARA items plus a score on the PCL-R.

Construction of an actuarial measure to determine risk of partner assault, specifically, was largely inspired by the success of the VRAG for gauging the risk of future wife assault in perpetrators of IPV (Hilton et al. 2001). In fact, it was entitled the DVRAG to reflect its connection with the VRAG (Hilton et al. 2008) and it shares many points to consider during the coding phase with its predecessors. For example, all of the instruments include measures of clinical history and the PCL-R (Hilton et al. 2010). The DVRAG demonstrated an early ability to discriminate between groups of high- and low-risk offenders during its standardization (Hilton et al. 2010). As noted by Hilton et al. (2010), the specific items include:

(1) *Number of prior domestic violence incidents*: This item covers all prior instances of physical assault by the perpetrator against a current/previous female cohabiting partner or her children. The incident must have occurred on a separate date before the index assault and must be recorded in a police report or criminal record;
(2) *Number of prior nondomestic incidents*: This includes physical assaults by the perpetrator against victims other than the current or previous female cohabiting partner or her children that occurred prior to the index assault;
(3) *Prior custodial sentence of 30 days or more*: This is scored if the offender has ever been sanctioned and incarcerated for at least 30 days prior to the index assault;

(4) *Failure on prior Conditional Release*: This item should be scored "No" if the offender was *not* on Conditional Release at the time of the index assault and/or has no history of failing to comply with Conditional Release conditions;
(5) *Threats to harm or kill at the index assault*: This item is scored if the perpetrator made threats to harm others during the time of the index assault. It may also be scored if the perpetrator was charged with threatening or an equivalent offense;
(6) *Confinement of the partner at the index assault*: This item should be scored positively if the perpetrator confined the victim to a locked area, a barricaded area, or physically prevented the victim from leaving during the index assault;
(7) *Victim concern*: This variable should be scored positive if the female victim of the index assault verbally stated that she was concerned, afraid, worried, or certain that the perpetrator would assault her or her children in the future;
(8) *Number of children*: This includes the number of living minor or adult biological or adopted children of the perpetrator, as well as the additional children of the victim;
(9) *Victim's biological children from a previous partner*: This item pertains to all the living minor or adult biological children of the female victim of the index assault, whose father is not the perpetrator. Adopted children should not be included;
(10) *Violence against others*: This is scored if the perpetrator has any nondomestic physical assaults prior to the index assault. The incident does not need to be officially recorded in a police report or Court documents;
(11) *Substance abuse score*: This variable is based on the number of factors present that indicate substance abuse concerns;
(12) *Assault on victim when pregnant*: This item is scored regardless of whether or not the incident is documented in a police report;
(13) *Number of barriers to victim support*: This item refers to the number of barriers present that interfere with the victim's access to support services; and,
(14) *Psychopathy Checklist-Revised (PCL-R) score*: As in other cases, a previously documented PCL-R score may be used if there is inadequate information available.

The evaluator scores the DVRAG according to a coding sheet that is provided. To begin with, the examiner goes through the list of possible scoring options and picks the ones most supported by the available information. The item scores are then tallied for a final total score. The possible range of scores on the DVRAG ranges from −10 to +46. The total score is translated using a table that is provided with the measure that indicates the perpetrator's probability of recidivism. The score and likelihood of recidivism can be used for safety planning, as well as for determining the intervention and resources necessary to prevent future violence (Hilton et al. 2010). Higher scores generally reflect greater risk, although the DVRAG cannot actually provide estimates regarding the likelihood of deadly assaults. However, the presence of additional factors may indicate increased reason for concern, such as use of firearms, the termination of the relationship, and/or the victim having a new partner (Hilton et al. 2010).

Static-99

The Static-99—so named to reflect the tool's rather singular focus on "static" variables—is a 10-item actuarial risk assessment instrument crafted to determine the level of risk for sexual and/or violent re-offending posed by adult male sexual offenders (Hanson and Thornton 1999). The offender must have already been convicted of at least one sexual offense against a non-consenting adult or child (Campbell 2007). It should not be used with offenders younger than 18 years of age at the time of release or with female offenders. The normative data used to interpret a respondent's score was updated in 2009 to include a wider variety of sex offenders and increase the instrument's generalizability (Helmus et al. 2009). Indeed, the Static-99 has been described by some as the most widely used (McGrath et al. 2010) and most empirically studied risk assessment instrument for use with adult male sexual offenders (Hanson and Morton-Bourgon 2009).

The Static-99 is composed of 10 items, which are scored using the 2003 revised coding rules (Harris et al. 2003). The measure solicits information from three areas in an offender's life: Demographic information, criminal history, and victim information (Harris et al. 2003, p. 11). Each of the items is listed with three elements attached, namely "The Basic Principle," "The Basic Rule," and a list of criteria to score the item (Harris et al. 2003, p. 1). Scores range from 0 to 12 and are used to determine an offender's placement into one of four risk categories, which reflects the respondent's long-term risk potential.

As previously indicated, the Static-99 is divided into three dimensions. The first, Demographic Information, is quite straightforward and includes the following items:

(1) *Youth*: This item asks if the offender will be between his 18th and 25th birthday at exposure to risk—In other words, will the offender be at least 18 years of age when released and, subsequently, given the chance to re-offend? Justification for inclusion of the item is based on research (Hanson 2001) reflecting that a younger age is related to an increased risk of recidivism. If the evaluation is looking at the potential for re-offending at a future point in time, the age at which he will be exposed to risk is used (Hanson and Thornton 2003); and,

(2) *Ever lived with an intimate partner—Two years*?: This item inquires whether or not the offender has ever lived with an intimate partner for at least 2 years. This item was selected based on Hanson and Bussiere's (1998) meta-analysis concerning risk factors for sexual recidivism. Ultimately, it is a reflection of whether the offender had the personality and resources needed to maintain a relatively stable relationship with another adult, regardless of whether it a heterosexual or homosexual relationship (Harris et al. 2003). The examiner must make sure that the quality of the relationship meets the criteria for the item, which includes a list of factors to be considered (e.g., extended absences). This is the only item on the tool that can be omitted if there is insufficient information available.

The second dimension on the Static-99 inquires about a number of factors related to criminal history. This section comes with a very comprehensive list of rules and exclusionary criteria for coding that should be reviewed prior to rating the assessment, especially since different interpretations of the items can lead to different outcomes. For example, it is possible for an offender to commit a number of sexual offenses in different jurisdictions over a protracted period—be it during a spree or spread out over many years—before finally being detected or arrested. When such is the case, the grouping of charges and convictions would constitute an "index cluster" rather than multiple index "offenses" (Harris et al. 2003). This is because the offender was not caught, sanctioned, and then chose to re-offend yet again after being released. The criminal history section includes the following items:

(3) *Index Nonsexual Violence—Any Convictions*?: This items asks if there was a conviction for a separate, nonsexually violent offense addressed on the same sentencing occasion as the index sex offense. It is based on research (Hanson and Bussiere 1998) indicating that a history of nonsexual violence is predictive of future violence, as well as the potential for serious injury if the individual does recidivate (Harris et al. 2003);

(4) *Prior Nonsexual Violence—Any Convictions*?: This item is similar to the previous item, but refers to any conviction that is not part of the index offense. Also like item #3, this item was included based on research (Hanson and Bussiere 1998) indicating that a history of nonsexual violence is, again, predictive of future violence and the potential for serious injury (Harris et al. 2003). It may also reflect difficulties with impulse control and an unwillingness (or inability to) conform their behavior, even after being disciplined;

(5) *Prior Sex Offenses*?: This item is used to identify patterns that reflect a higher likelihood of future re-offending. It includes both *prior* charges and convictions, which are summed separately; charges that were dropped or did not result in a conviction are also included. After the number of charges and convictions has been totaled, the raw scores are converted to final scores. The highest final score is the score that is recorded. The index offense is not included when tallying the final score for this item (Harris et al. 2003);

(6) *Prior Sentencing Dates*?: This item seeks to establish a pattern of criminal behavior by asking if the offender has either had four or more or less than four sentencing dates prior to the index offense (Harris et al. 2003). Ultimately, it is asking if the offender can be deterred by a fear of the consequences; and,

(7) *Any Convictions for Noncontact Sex Offenses*?: This item involves offenses such as voyeurism and exhibitionism. It was included based on the rationale that most individuals have little interest in exposing themselves to strangers, stealing underwear, etc. (Harris et al. 2003). The authors also note that offenders who engage in these types of behaviors are more likely to have problems altering their behavior to match conventional standards (Harris et al. 2003). Ultimately, it reflects the likelihood of the offender modifying his maladaptive sexual behavior.

The final portion of the Static-99 is referred to as "The Three Victim Questions." Not surprisingly, this section addresses the offender's choice of victims. It is important to note that these items do not apply to nonsexual offenses or sexual offenses relating to prostitution, offenses against animals, possession of child pornography, and public sex with consenting adults (Harris et al. 2003). The items for this section include:

(8) *Any Unrelated Victims*?: The manual cites research (i.e., Harris and Hanson, unpublished manuscript) demonstrating that offenders who only aggress against those who are related to them are less likely to re-offend than individuals who offend against those they are not related to. A victim is considered to be related if the relationship is sufficiently close that marriage would be prohibited. Additional criteria needed to determine relatedness are provided in the coding manual (Harris et al. 2003);

(9) *Any Stranger Victims*?: This item (Harris et al. 2003) is very similar to the one preceding it, but it more specifically reflects whether the offender is driven enough to seek out a target who cannot identify him so that he can avoid detection; and,

(10) *Any Male Victims*?: This item is based on research suggesting that offenders who victimize males are more likely to re-offend in the future than offenders who exclusively victimize females (Hanson and Bussiere 1998). This includes non-consenting adults and children.

In terms of coding, the evaluator should rely on information that can be corroborated by outside sources. Scoring the items based on self-report is strongly discouraged, yet some flexibility is allowed. For example, if it is impossible to obtain file information or access collateral sources, some limited usage of self-report is acceptable; however, the information needs to seem credible and reasonable to the evaluator (Harris et al. 2003). The specific information needed to score the Static-99 depends on which of the three categories is being assessed (Harris et al. 2003). According to the coding manual, the demographic items can be scored using information derived from official records or collateral sources. Regarding the offender's criminal history, the evaluator must have access to the official criminal record. For the items addressing an offender's victim selection, the use of all credible information is recommended, including self-report, victim and/or witness statements, and third-party sources.

The evaluator may begin scoring the Static-99 after the requisite information has been gathered. This phase is completed on a coding sheet that is provided. As with the previously mentioned instruments, a rating is given after the evaluator has looked through the response options and selected that which is most supported by the available information. To determine the total score for the measure, the evaluator simply sums the scores for each of the individual items. Again, total scores can range from 0 to 12 and reflect estimates of future risk based on the number of risk factors present in any one individual (Harris et al. 2003). In general, the more risk factors the offender endorses, the more likely he is to recidivate in the future (e.g., Austin et al. 2003).

After the total score for the Static-99 has been calculated, the evaluator consults the table entitled, "Static-99 Recidivism Percentages by Risk Level," which includes recidivism risk estimates for both sexual and violent recidivism over 5-, 10-, and 15-year periods (Harris et al. 2003). The evaluator notes the specific recidivism rates (the more recent norms should be used for more geographically diverse populations). Although the tool is useful for estimating long-term risk potential (Conroy and Murrie 2007), it is not possible to determine specifically when he will recidivate.

As was the case with the previously discussed actuarial measures, the Static-99's development was retrospective in design and based on facts readily available in database records. The risk factors were first identified during a review of the empirical literature, after which statistical analyses were performed to determine which risk factors made the greatest contributions (Hanson and Thornton 1999).

A modified version of the Static-99 was later developed and, not surprisingly, it was entitled the Static-2002 (Hanson and Thornton 2003). This measure is unique from the Static-99 because it includes some theoretically meaningful variables thought to drive sexual offender recidivism (Phenix et al. 2008). Both measures were then revised, resulting in the development of the Static-99R and Static-2002R (Helmus et al. 2011). Both instruments are essentially identical to the predecessors, but with one major modification: The effect of aging on recidivism is taken into account to minimize overestimation of recidivism risk in older offenders. Thus, the item addressing an offender's age at release is weighted differently and, therefore, each response option is assigned a different point value than that which is assigned in the original instruments (Helmus et al. 2012). This is the only item for which the effect of aging is reflected.

Coding the Static-99R and Static-2002R entails the same process that was used with the other instruments. Basically, the rating is completed on a coding sheet that is provided, the most supported option is selected, and the total score is simply a summation of all individual item scores. On the Static-99R, 0 to 1 is considered Low risk; 2 to 3 is deemed a Moderate-Low risk; 4 to 5 is listed as a Moderate-High risk; and values of 6 or greater are regarded as High risk (Helmus et al. 2011). On the Static-2002R, a score that is less than or equal to 2 is classified as Low risk; a score of 3 or 4 reflects a Moderate-Low risk; a score of 5 or 6 indicates Moderate risk; a score of 7 or 8 suggests Moderate-High risk; and a value of 9 or greater is regarded as High risk (Helmus et al. 2011). Hanson et al. (2012) made available a systematic method for relaying these results, namely percentile ranks, to minimize ambiguity.

Rapid Risk Assessment for Sex Offender Recidivism (RRASOR)

The RRASOR is an actuarial risk assessment instrument designed to determine the level of risk posed by adult males who have already been convicted of at least one sexual offense (Hanson 1997). It was designed to be a brief instrument for identifying offenders who are at high risk for sexual re-offending. Indeed, this particular measure is quite useful for settings that entail routine screening of sex offenders. Hanson (1997) has noted, though, that it should only be used as a screening instrument to place offenders into relative risk levels until a more comprehensive assessment can be performed. Thus, the RRASOR should never be used in place of a more comprehensive measure. Like the other tools described thus far, the measure was not crafted for use with offenders who are less than 18 years of age or female offenders.

As previously indicated, there are only four items on the RRASOR (each of which is also found on the Static-99). These risk factors were selected from Hanson and Bussiere's (1996) meta-analysis concerning risk markers for sexual recidivism. Namely, the instrument includes: (1) Prior Sexual Offenses; (2) Being Between the Ages of 18 and 25 years Old; (3) Victim Gender; and (4) Any Unrelated Victims.

Coding the RRASOR is fairly straightforward. The first item, for instance, necessitates a simple summation based on the number of arrests or the number of convictions in an offender's criminal record. Like the Static-99, whichever option produces the higher score is selected for the final tally. It is important to note that this item is the most heavily weighted item on the RRASOR (Hanson 1997), which is not surprising as the best predictor of future behavior is past behavior. Only official records should be used to code this item. The second item, which addresses the offender's age, is based on the time of first opportunity to offend. The third item, victim gender, requires a review of all available information, including the offender's self-report, official records, collateral sources, and case notes (Hanson 1997). The final item, relationship to victim, includes spouses and family members who are too closely related to get married. Similarly, if the offender is in a caretaker role in the same house as the victim, they are also considered related (Hanson 1997). The evaluator scores on a provided coding sheet and must, of course, go through each of the possible scoring options. Total scores range from 0 to 6 with 10-year estimates concerning the likelihood of recidivism.

The items evaluated during the instrument's development were drawn from Hanson and Bussiere's (1996) meta-analysis concerning risk markers for sexual recidivism. An item was identified for consideration if it demonstrated a strong correlation with sexual recidivism and could be scored using commonly available information (Hanson 1997). Items were then either ruled-out or selected for inclusion in the final instrument based on the results of regression analyses using six samples of sexual offenders (Hanson 1997). The four items selected were identified as the best combination to most accurately predict the outcome of sexual recidivism in a brief amount of time; The items were then weighted according to their ability to predict the likelihood of recidivism over periods of 5–10 years (Hanson 1997).

Minnesota Sex Offender Screening Tool—Revised (MnSOST-R)

The MnSOST-R is an actuarial risk assessment instrument designed to assess the level of risk for sexual re-offending in adult male rapists and extra-familial child molesters who are incarcerated (Epperson et al. 2003). It was not designed for use with juveniles, females, offenders on probation, or intra-familial child molesters. Often, it is regarded as a screening tool for referral for commitment under Minnesota's Sexual Psychopathic Personality and Sexually Dangerous Persons Law (Epperson et al. 2003). The measure covers both static and dynamic variables (this is the only one of the actuarial instruments that makes specific reference to "dynamic" variables). Its predecessor, the Minnesota Sex Offender Screening Tool, had some clinical observations built in but the current revised version has variables based only on actuarial data (Conroy and Murrie 2007).

The MnSOST-R consists of a total of 16 items. The first 12 items are regarded as "Historical/Static variables" and the last four are considered the "Institutional/Dynamic Variables." The items identified for review by Epperson et al. (2003) are as follows:

(1) Number of sex/sex-related convictions (including current conviction);
(2) Length of sexual offending history;
(3) Was the offender under any form of supervision when s/he committed any sex offense for which they was eventually charged of convicted?;
(4) Was any sex offense (charged or convicted) committed in a public place?;
(5) Was force or the threat of force ever used to achieve compliance in any sex offense (charged or convicted)?;
(6) Did any sex offense (charged or convicted) involve multiple acts on a single victim within any single contact event?;
(7) Number of different age groups victimized across all sex/sex-related offenses (charged or convicted). The age groups of victims include 6 and younger; 7–12; 13–15, and the offender is more than 5 years older than the victim; and 16 and older;
(8) Offended against a 13–15-year-old victim and the offender was more than 5 years older than the victim at the time of the offense (charged or convicted);
(9) Was the victim a stranger in any sex/sex-related offense (charged or convicted);
(10) Is there evidence of adolescent antisocial behavior in the file?;
(11) Pattern of substantial drug or alcohol abuse (12 months prior to arrest for instant offense or revocation); and,
(12) Employment history (12 months prior to the arrest for instant offense or revocation).
(13) Discipline history while incarcerated;
(14) Chemical dependency treatment while incarcerated;
(15) Sex offender treatment history while incarcerated; and,
(16) Age of offender at time of release.

The scoring instructions, which were revised by Epperson et al. (2005), direct the evaluator to review the offender's file prior to assessment. Only information documented in official data sources should be used to score the instrument. Self-report information may be included on certain items (i.e., items 2, 10, 11 and 12), but only if it is already documented and determined to be reliable (Epperson et al. 2005). Offenses that were charged but not convicted are included if there is evidence that a sex offense was, in fact, attempted or perpetrated (Epperson et al. 2005).

The MnSOST-R was developed with a focus on making the instrument relatively easy to score to ensure that correctional personnel could use it effectively (Hoberman 2001). Scoring the MnSOST-R is fairly straightforward, in that the evaluator is tasked with identifying the response option best supported by the available information, selecting said item, and eventually tallying all item scores together to produce a total score (Epperson et al. 2003). As far as interpretation, an offender can be placed into one of three risk categories based on his score. Namely, a score of 3 or below is designated as Low (or Level 1); 4–7 is classified as Medium (or Level 2); and a score of 8 or above is regarded as High (or Level 3) (Epperson et al. 2003).

The items on the MnSOST-R were derived using information available in the Minnesota Department of Corrections offender files, which have been described as more comprehensive and detailed compared to the file information readily available in other states (e.g., DeClue 2002). As a result, the measure's inter-rater reliability has been described as very low because information necessary to score some of the items may not be available in an offender's file if he resides in a state other than Minnesota (Austin et al. 2003). After an item was selected for inclusion in the final instrument, each answer was weighted in accordance with its purported ability to predict sexual recidivism (Epperson et al. 2003). As noted before, the revised version was derived from empirical methods rather than clinical observation to ensure improved predictive validity (Epperson et al. 2003).

Structured Professional Judgment

The instruments to be described in this section are not actuarial, at least in the sense that the previously described tools were. Rather, they utilize structured professional judgment (SPJ) methodology. Structured Professional Judgment—or, as it is sometimes called, structured clinical judgment—attempts to combine all of the psychological research regarding violent or sexually violent offending into a series of distinct categories, and then uses a structured interview format to ensure all areas are adequately covered. Therefore, unlike the actuarial approach, there is a good deal of leeway for clinical judgment and clinical interview; However, the areas covered are very carefully derived from the available research. Some authors regard it as an amalgamation of the actuarial and clinical methods.

Historical, Clinical, Risk Management-20 (HCR-20)

The first instrument that we will discuss within this category is the Historical, Clinical, Risk Management-20 (HCR-20) scheme, Version 2 (Webster et al. 1997). The HCR-20 is a SPJ scheme "intended to be used to guide a comprehensive, structured assessment of violence risk for adults (18+) within forensic psychiatric, civil psychiatric and offender samples" (Douglas et al. 2014). This measure is basically a formalized guide for the systematic assessment and management of violence risk. (Conroy and Murrie 2007) and represents one of the first attempts to join clinical methods of assessment with the available research on the prediction of violence (Webster et al. 1997). For the purposes of the HCR-20, violence is defined as "actual, attempted, or threatened harm to a person of persons" (Webster et al. 1997).

The HCR-20 is comprised of 20 items that address historical (H), clinical (C), and risk management (R) factors. It considers dynamic risk factors and, in that way, differs from most of the actuarial assessment instruments. Unlike the MnSOST-R, which is the only actuarial that makes reference to "dynamic" variables, these factors are not limited to behavior in an institution. Such an approach is useful for monitoring change in risk status over time and, for this reason, it can be useful for case management and treatment planning (Webster et al. 1997).

The HCR-20 assesses the risk for future violence by providing a review of three specific areas in an individual's life: his/her past and present behavior, as well as potential future circumstances. Past behavior, specifically, is captured by the Historical scale. The items in this section are often given the greatest weight because they are, technically, actuarial risk factors (Borum 2007). In other words, these items are listed on many of the actuarial measures and their utility has already been discussed in the literature. Despite the overlap, there is more of a "clinical feel" to these items than in the actuarial assessments. The Clinical scale, on the other hand, is far more individually oriented, as well as more suited for determining short term-risk of violence (e.g., inpatient violence; McNeil et al. 2003) and treatment implications. Finally, situational factors that can occur post-treatment are found on the Risk Management scale. These items prompt a proactive evaluation of future circumstances to minimize risk of relapse/decompensation. The manual notes that it may be helpful to consult with those responsible for treatment or community release when completing this section (Webster et al. 1997). The specific HCR-20 items are as follows:
Historical:

(H1) Previous violence;
(H2) Young age at first violent incident;
(H3) Relationship instability;
(H4) Employment problems;
(H5) Substance use problems;
(H6) Major mental illness;
(H7) Psychopathy;

(H8) Early maladjustment;
(H9) Personality disorder; and,
(H10) Prior supervision failure.

Clinical:

(C1) Lack of insight;
(C2) Negative attitudes;
(C3) Active symptoms of major mental illness;
(C4) Impulsivity; and,
(C5) Lack of responsiveness to treatment.

Risk Management:

(R1) Future plans lack feasibility;
(R2) Exposure to destabilizers;
(R3) Lack of personal support;
(R4) Noncompliance with remediation attempts; and,
(R5) Stress.

The coding process for the HCR-20 was "cloned from the PCL-R" (Cawood and Corcoran 2009), meaning it utilizes a similar three-point system. Specifically, a score of 0 is assigned if the risk factor is not present or is contraindicated by the available information; a 1 if the available information suggests the possible presence or mild presence of an item; and a score of 2 if the available information definitely indicates the item's presence (Webster et al. 1997). If there is insufficient information to code an item, the evaluator is given the option to omit that item (Arbisi 2003). Each item is concretely defined in the manual to provide clarity. As in the PCL-R, multiple sources of information are needed in order to adequately assess the presence of each risk factor.

Scoring the HCR-20 is completed on a coding sheet provided. According to Webster et al. (1997), there is little sense in using random fixed cutoff scores to determine an individual's placement into a risk category. Rather than merely summing the scores (as was done with the actuarials), it is recommended that the evaluator use the information to assign the examinee to a risk classification level—Low, Moderate, or High—based on the number of risk factors present in the specific individual being assessed (Webster et al. 1997). Also, in contrast with actuarial methodology, reliance on group-based scores is discouraged.

Again, the HCR-20 is an example of structured professional judgment, rather than an actuarial instrument. It was designed to establish whether or not certain important risk factors are present in a respondent (like, a checklist) rather than produce a numerical summation. Thus, it is recommended that the results be listed as risk and protective factors rather than numbers because numerical results could be misleading (Webster et al. 1997). The authors further note that there are certain items that, on their own, could render and individual at high risk for future violence. For example, the items concerning substance abuse, psychopathy, poor insight, difficulty inhibiting one's behavior, and noncompliance with remediation could be ominous indicators. Again, it is obvious that clinical judgment plays a significant role in interpreting these various factors.

Sexual Violence Risk-20 (SVR-20)

The SVR-20 is an example of structured professional judgment designed to identify individuals at risk of committing sexual violence (Boer et al. 1997). Like the HCR-20, this instrument assists in the systematic review of critical factors (many of which are shared by the two instruments); however, the SVR-20 also contains certain risk factors that are more specific to sexual offending. It also allows the individual examiner to, once again, pursue each of the variables using their own clinical judgment.

As noted above, the SVR-20 is a list of structured professional judgment guidelines that highlight variables in an offender's life to explore during a thorough assessment. The SVR-20 includes items that address three areas in an offender's life: Psychosocial adjustment, sexual offenses, and future plans (Boer et al. 1997). The SVR-20 also includes psychophysiological data, such as penile plethysmographic evaluation. The specific items include:

A. Psychosocial adjustment:

(1) Sexual deviation;
(2) Victim of child abuse;
(3) Psychopathy;
(4) Major mental illness;
(5) Substance abuse problems;
(6) Suicidal/homicidal ideation;
(7) Relationship problems;
(8) Employment problems;
(9) Past nonsexual violent offenses;
(10) Past nonviolent offenses; and,
(11) Past supervision failure.

B. Sexual offenses:

(12) High-density sex offenses;
(13) Multiple sex offense types;
(14) Physical harm to victim;
(15) Use of weapons or threats of death in sex offenses;
(16) Escalation in frequency or severity of sex offenses;
(17) Extreme minimization or denials of sex offenses; and,
(18) Attitudes that support or condone sex offenses.

C. Future Plans:

(19) Lacks realistic plans; and,
(20) Negative attitude toward intervention.

There is an additional section on the SVR-20, entitled "Other Considerations," that does not include any items to be coded. Rather, it may be used to document unique risk factors and idiographic data that may have influenced the final judgment regarding level of risk (Boer et al. 1997).

Barbaree et al. (2008) reported that including information about an offender's age-at-release can improve the measure's predictive accuracy. More specifically, they found that 13 out of the 20 items on the SVR-20 reflect a general anti-social lifestyle and, when age was corrected for, there was a subsequent reduction each item's predictive power. These items include: (2) Victim of child abuse; (3) Psychopathy; (5) Substance abuse problems; (6) Suicidal or homicidal ideation; (7) Relationship problems; (8) Employment problems; (9) Past nonsexual violent offenses; (10) Past nonviolent offenses; (11) Past supervision failure; (14) Physical harm to victims; (15) Use of weapons or threats of death in sex offenses; (19) Lack of realistic plans; and (20) Negative attitude toward intervention. In short, increasing age diminishes the power of these variables to predict recidivism.

Scoring the SVR-20 is very similar to the process used with the HCR-20: 0 (factor not present), 1 (partially or possibly present), and 2 (definitely present) (Boer et al. 1997). Also like the HCR-20, all available information—including interviews, criminal records, prior mental health reports, the results of standardized psychological measures, and psychophysiological data—should be used when rating the items (Budrionis 2003). If the available information indicates that a risk factor is not applicable to the offender, the examiner moves on to the next item in the list.

As noted in the discussion of the HCR-20, a summation of the individual item scores is not optimal for interpretation. Rather, the SVR-20 should be used as a set of guidelines to determine which information from an offender's history should be considered in order to assign the examinee to a risk classification level of Low, Moderate, or High (Boer et al. 1997).

Spousal Assault Risk Assessment Guide (SARA)

The SARA is a structured professional judgment scheme developed as a clinical guide to evaluate the level of risk posed by perpetrators of intimate partner violence toward partners or ex-partners, children, other family members, and other possible targets (Kropp et al. 1999). The SARA also provides a structured way of reviewing important information and is useful for violence prevention and correctional decisions (Bourgon 2011); it can also be used to determine case management strategies and interventions (Bowen 2011). The 20 items function as a sort of checklist that results in two overall risk estimates: imminent risk of violence toward the partner or ex-partner and imminent risk of violence toward others. However, there is no clear definition of what constitutes "imminent" (Helmus and Bourgon 2011).

The 20 items on the SARA address both static and dynamic risk factors and are broken down into four sections: criminal history, psychosocial adjustment, spousal assault history and current/most recent offense (index offense) (Kropp et al. 1999). There is a final section, "Other Considerations," where idiographic risk factors that contributed to the overall judgment can be noted (e.g., stalking). The items are as follows:

A. Criminal History:

(1) Past assault of family members;
(2) Past assault of strangers or acquaintances; and,
(3) Past violation of Conditional Release or community supervision.

B. Psychosocial Adjustment:

(4) Recent relationship problems;
(5) Recent employment problems;
(6) Victim of and/or witness to family violence as a child or adolescent;
(7) Recent substance abuse or dependence;
(8) Recent suicidal or homicidal ideation or intent;
(9) Recent psychotic or manic symptoms; and,
(10) Personality disorder with anger, impulsivity or behavioral instability.

C. Spousal Assault History:

(11) Past physical assault;
(12) Past sexual assault/sexual jealousy;
(13) Past use of weapons and/or credible threats of death;
(14) Recent escalation in frequency or severity of assault;
(15) Past violation of No Contact Orders;
(16) Extreme minimization or denial of spousal assault history; and,
(17) Items that support or condone spousal assault.

D. Current/most recent offenses:

(18) Severe and/or sexual assault;
(19) Use of weapons and/or credible threats of death; and,
(20) Violation of No Contact Order.

The scoring process for the SARA is similar to that used for the HCR-20 and SVR-20. Thus, a score of 0, 1, or 2 is awarded for each item based on its applicability (Kropp et al. 1999). After the SARA has been scored and the presence of critical items noted, the evaluator makes a final determination of whether the perpetrator is Low, Moderate, or High risk. This segment is referred to as the "summary risk judgment" and results in two possible scores. The first score covers imminent risk of harm to the spouse and the second score addresses imminent risk of harm to another identifiable person (Kropp et al. 1999). As with the other SPJ tools, a simple summation of the item values is discouraged.

The SARA was one of the first measures designed specifically for determining risk of IPV (Hilton et al. 2010), and is frequently described as the most well-research measure for interpersonal violence (Hilton and Harris 2007). Development of the SARA began with a review of the literature to identify traits and behavior patterns that could discriminate between IPV perpetrators who would re-offend from those who would not (Kropp et al. 1995). Clinical and legal factors were also considered during the item selection process (Kropp and Hart 2000). The normative data were obtained using two groups of adult male offenders, namely offenders on probation and inmates. While all of these subjects had a history of interpersonal violence, not all were incarcerated or on probation for that reason (Katz 2003).

Observations and Limitations

Risk assessment measures, whether actuarial in nature or relying on structured professional judgment, typically have one major element in common: They produce results that are only slightly better than chance. This level seems to hold regardless of whether we are talking about sexual recidivism or violent recidivism Truly, it is not uncommon for studies concerning the predictive validity of risk assessment tools to produce results that conflict with the findings of other studies. Clearly, this is an exceedingly complex area and within this brief overview we cannot discuss these in any great detail. However, a few general comments are in order.

Sampling error. First, let us look at the issue of sampling error. Sampling error is a term used in statistics to refer to discrepancies between the characteristics of a sample chosen to represent a population, as well as when findings are generalized despite it being inappropriate to do so. When we look at the predictive ability of risk assessment instruments, sampling error frequently comes into play and occurs when different groups of sexual offenders or violent offenders are assumed to represent all such offenders. For example, a study that utilizes a sample composed of rapists to determine the predictive validity of a risk assessment instrument for sex offenders is unlikely to produce the same results as would be obtained from a sample of child molesters. This is because the risk factors that predict recidivism in rapists are often distinct from the risk factors that predict sexual re-offending in child molesters (Firestone et al. 2000; Hanson and Morton-Bourgon 2005). Given that these instruments are an amalgam of risk factors, some of which may be more applicable for one sex offender subtype than other, it is not surprising that they have only moderate predictive validity, at best. It may be wiser to construct assessment instruments that measure for specific sex offender subtypes than to continue relying on a "one size fits all" approach.

Even the kinds of predictions made may vary. Becker (2014), in a presentation at the APA-ABA conference on Violence and the Family, noted that certain risk factors may predict violence in general, while others may predict an initial sexual offense, while still others may predict sexual recidivism; According to Becker, far more research needs to be done to "fine-tune" the assessments and exactly what they do predict. Becker further notes that no one etiological theory is widely accepted. Some theories include, but are not limited to, brain structure, hormonal abnormalities, cognitive distortions, distorted social learning and conditioning, and a variety of personality variables. She notes that Antisocial Personality Disorder *is* a risk factor for those who will rape, but not for those who engage in child molestation. In short, according to Becker, sex offenders are a heterogeneous group, have no distinct profile, and come from all walks of life. She suggests that future research follow a model that widens the range of both predictor and criterion variables being studied. Becker further suggests that future research needs to include biological predispositions, family and peer group influences, and the individual's capacity for self-regulation. She notes, for instance, that not all child molesters or rapists have a paraphilic disorder, nor do all diagnosed with a paraphilic disorder have offense histories. Incest offenders tend to have fewer victims, and extra-familial sex offenders are more likely to have deviant sexual preferences. Noncontact offenders, such as voyeurs, exhibitionists, and Internet offenders, tend to show more elements of compulsivity and a larger number of victims.

Treatment versus no prior treatment. Another area has to do with offenders with a history of treatment, as opposed to those with no prior treatment. An offender's history of treatment may pose additional issues. There are many studies that have used offenders with a history of treatment or currently in treatment while others used offenders with no history of treatment. Clearly, some factors may apply in one group that would not apply in another, and certainly in other areas where there is a purported use of so-called "dynamic variables," the nature of their participation in treatment is not even included. Also, the nature of the treatment needs to be examined as the different orientations encourage different approaches.

Ethnic differences. An offender's ethnicity has also been found to influence the outcome of a study examining an instrument's predictive validity. For instance, Varela et al. (2013) found that the Static-99 (and Static-99R) were far less effective in predicting sexual re-offending with Latino offenders than they were with African-Americans and Caucasians. It may well be premature to assume that these tools are equally predictive across the ethnicities. A frequent occurrence, as observed in court by one of the authors (D.S.), is the tendency of forensic examiners to either be oblivious to these findings or just dismissive of them.

Location. The country in which the study took place has also been found to influence the reported predictive ability of an instrument. In a meta-analysis examining the accuracy of assessment measures for identifying an offender's risk of sexual re-offending, Hanson and Morton-Bourgon (2009) determined that the effect sizes produced by such instruments were strongest in the United Kingdom and rather weak in the United States. Since the majority of the assessments were derived in Canada and the United Kingdom, this is not particularly surprising since the United States has a more diverse ethnic make-up. Additional research is needed to determine whether these differences are or are not exclusively attributable to ethnic differences.

Research validity versus field validity. Research validity describes how valid a measure is when applied by researchers who have received training in the administration and coding of the assessment. Field validity has to do with the predictive validity of the same measure when administered and scored by clinicians. Often, the research validity surpasses the field validity because the researchers have greater familiarity with the operational definitions and coding criteria used during a tool's development. Murrie et al. (2012), for instance, found this to be the case in some of their evaluators scoring the PCL-R. Similarly, in one recent study (Singh et al. 2013) it was found that studies authored by an instrument's designers reported predictive validity rates almost twice a high as those found by independent researchers. They identified this as a result of "authorship bias."

Operational definitions of recidivism. Another factor that may relate to the applicability of a study has to do with the definition of recidivism. Some studies may define recidivism as a new arrest, a new charge, or a new conviction. Therefore, it stands to reason that much of the research reportedly evaluating for the same general outcome is really looking at different things. An examiner must keep these details in mind before generalizing the findings of any study.

Actuarial scoring of Structured Professional Judgment measures. A validity issue unique to structured professional judgment studies relates to the way in which the instrument was coded. Structured professional judgment, as noted above, generally produces summary risk ratings rather than absolute actuarial scores. Nevertheless, a good portion of the literature regarding structured professional judgment's validity is based on studies that did not score the instrument according to how it was designed. According to Hanson and Morton-Bourgon (2007), this basically results in the measure being transformed from a structured professional judgment measure to a "conceptual actuarial measure" (p. 3). Therefore, it would be inappropriate to generalize the validity reported by such studies to that which might be found if the instrument were coded as intended, as it introduces sampling error.

Inter-rater reliability. Although structured professional judgment measures were not intended to be actuarially scored, the benefit of such an approach could be improved inter-rater reliability, as summary risk judgments are often based on informed clinical judgment, which may, in fact, vary from one examiner to another. Certain examiners using the SARA, for instance, may give extra weight to stalking behavior endorsed by a perpetrator of interpersonal violence, while a different examiner may not. If such is the case, different summary risk ratings may be expected.

Base rate issues. Going back to the early work on risk assessment, Monahan observed that base rate data in frequently missing in these circumstances and, therefore, any statistics regarding likelihood of offending cannot be truly put within context. The results of an assessment are often adjusted to reflect the number of offenders that recidivate in a particular area. Such estimates may be inaccurate because sexual and violent offense frequently go unreported. In fact, the U.S. Department of Justice (2014), in their annual survey concerning criminal victimization, found that fewer than half of those who experienced violent victimization (46 %) and sexual assault victimizations (35 %) reported it to the police. Overall, low or inaccurate base rates inevitably create issues for the accuracy of violence risk assessment measures (Szmukler 2001).

Group versus individual data. As noted before, one of the major concerns is that the actuarial approach will only point to the fact that the individual belongs to a group that has a particular likelihood of re-offending. It does not say whether or not that particular individual will re-offend, with the latter estimate needing to be made based on idiographic and clinical data. Therefore, while there are many claims that the actuarial approach is superior to the clinical approach, this really omits the fact that the current approach to risk assessment is primarily that of structured professional or structured clinical judgment, not the unaided clinical judgment that was used previously. It is, in fact, remarkable that textbooks and presentations at meetings still use the artificial distinction between actuarial (the scientific) and unaided clinical (the nonscientific) approach in order to make their assertions. The concept of structured professional judgment as representing an amalgamation of the best in both areas appears to be sorely lacking.

Another area desperately in need of more research is the interactive effect of various risk factors. Dvoskin (2014) in the APA/ABA conference on Violence and the Family, noted the misperception propagated by the media: That mental illness and violence are highly correlated. In fact, only 5 to 10 % of violent crime can be attributed to severe mental illness alone; while most mentally ill individuals do not act violently, they often have other risk factors such as child abuse, victimization, unemployment, and substance abuse; co-occurrence with substance abuse, for instance, is known to multiply the base rate by a factor of 3. Dvoskin also notes a high correlation between those few mentally ill individuals who do act violently and suicidal ideation/behavior on their parts. He recommends doing a suicide risk assessment as part of any violence risk assessment. Clearly, a more complex analysis, such as the MacArthur studies, needs to be utilized on a widespread basis.

Chapter 3
Clinical Practice

Having looked at the historical background and the specific methods for performing risk assessments, let us now turn to how this is translated into clinical practice. These are sometimes called "Duty to Warn" or "Duty to Protect" third parties. We will examine them to see what the courts seem to be interpreting as appropriate standards to follow. We will assume for the moment that most readers are familiar with the legal history of most of these cases, so they will only be described in very general terms. What will be stressed is how the courts seem to conceptualize the standards of care in such cases. We will only consider cases in which the courts did weigh in on these concepts.

Tarasoff v. Regents of the University of California (1976)

Most people are aware of this case, in which the first decision was handed down in 1974. Prosenjit Poddar, a student at the University of California at Berkeley, confided in his therapist that he was planning to kill the woman he regarded as his girlfriend, a young woman named Tatiana Tarasoff. His therapist was concerned about this threat and notified the Campus Police in an effort to have Poddar involuntarily committed. The police did not think Poddar was an imminent risk, believed he was "rational," and did not detain him. The therapist, who was very concerned about this, consulted with his supervisor and was told that nothing further could be done. Several months later, Poddar did, in fact, kill Tatiana Tarasoff.

The family filed a law suit against the Regents of the University of California, putting forward a new cause of action, called duty to warn: Essentially, they argued that when the police failed to detain Poddar, the therapist had a duty to warn the intended victim (thereby breaking confidentiality). The trial court dismissed the case and the family appealed. The American Psychiatric Association filed an Amicus Curiae (which, when translated, means "friend of the court") brief arguing against a duty to warn, stating that it not only would water down the concept of confidentiality in psychotherapy, it would also involve unreliable predictions of the potential for future violence.

D.L. Shapiro and A.M. Noe, *Risk Assessment*,
SpringerBriefs in Behavioral Criminology, DOI 10.1007/978-3-319-17058-9_3

In 1976, the California Supreme Court issued what is now sometimes referred to as "Tarasoff II." In this opinion, the court broadened the "duty to warn" to a "duty to protect." It stated that when a therapist becomes aware of a threat made to an identifiable third party by a patient of theirs, the therapist must take "reasonable steps" to protect that intended victim from such violent behavior. It is important to note that, in contrast to the original "duty to warn," the court was now leaving the intervention to be taken up to the therapist's discretion. According to the court, the protective privilege ended where the public peril began. Therapists are not expected to do anything different from their standard practice which of course should always include careful assessments leading to appropriate interventions. The court did not suggest what the reasonable steps were, but many authors have subsequently talked about a variety of alternatives: increasing the number of therapy sessions, giving the patient access to an emergency number to call, placing the patient on medication, increasing or changing medication, considering voluntary or involuntary hospitalization, bringing the intended victim into the therapy session, and as a last resort, notifying the intended victim or police authorities.

The important point is that each therapist, when a threat is made, must conduct a careful assessment to determine, given the circumstances, what the appropriate intervention might be, one that is consistent with or logically flow from, the assessment. Of course, careful documentation and consultation with colleagues would also be considered important steps to take. Liability would derive from not doing a careful assessment, rather than from failure to accurately predict the future. If a careful assessment is done, and the intervention logically derives from the assessment, the therapist would not be found negligent. Negligence would mean that the therapist did not do an assessment or if they did one, that it was not consistent with the standards of the profession in doing such evaluations.

In summary, looking at the Tarasoff case in terms of risk assessment principles, the threat had been communicated to the therapist, and referred to an identifiable third party; the duty is discharged if the therapist follows a standard of care in doing an assessment. It does not have to be a specific kind of assessment, but it must be consistent with some accepted body of scientific or professional literature. Of interest is the fact that Poddar, at one time, roomed with the brother of Tatiana Tarasoff and confided in him his violent fantasies. No liability was ever considered for the brother since he did not have a "special relationship" with the patient, conceptualized legally (rightly or wrongly) as the ability to exert control over the patient's behavior.

McIntosh v. Milano (1979)

This was a 1979 case from the state of New Jersey, in which a psychiatrist was sued by the family of a woman who was killed by her boyfriend, a patient of the psychiatrist. The young man had a serious drug problem, and when he and his girlfriend had disagreements, he would engage in mischievous destructive behaviors, such as letting the air out of her tires and firing a BB gun at the windows of her car when she was not in it; however, when under the influence of drugs, he had violent fantasies directed toward his girlfriend, though he never acted on them. He stole a prescription pad from his psychiatrist, forged a signature, and had the prescription filled. By the time the psychiatrist got around to contacting his patient, the young man had already acted out and killed his girlfriend. The plaintiff's expert opined that in this case the violence was not speculation, but rather was a known fact. This expert was of the opinion that the property damage mischief coupled with the violent fantasies was an unambiguous warning signal, seeing it as an escalation that would eventually and predictably lead to violence by the young man against his girlfriend.

While this case was not summarily dismissed, as Dr. Milano had wished, the jury found the doctor not negligent, believing that the mischief plus violent fantasies when on drugs were not the same as an actual intention to do bodily harm. Therefore, the most important lesson to be taken from this case is for a jury to find a doctor negligent, it would have to be convinced that a threat was communicated to the therapist, that it involved an identifiable third party, and that it was clear and unambiguous. The idea of the therapist having to put together the "pieces of a puzzle" was not regarded as part of the standard of care in doing these assessments.

Shaw v. Glickman (1980)

This case, in the state of Maryland, was on one level, very simple and on another more complex. It involved a therapist who had in his group, a woman, her estranged husband, and unbeknownst to that therapist another man who happened to be the wife's paramour. The husband "put two and two together," figured out the relationship of his estranged wife and the other man and shot both of them while they were in bed. The paramour then sued the therapist for failure to warn him of the husband's violent tendencies.

The simple part of this case was that Maryland had no Duty to Warn statute at that point in time, so legally there was no basis for the lawsuit. The more intriguing aspect from a risk assessment perspective is whether the husband's history of anger, coupled with his apparent recognition that his estranged wife and the other man in the group were having an affair, was sufficient to trigger any need on the part of the therapist to protect an intended victim, or whether the scenario, coupled with a past history of jealous anger, should have prompted the therapist, once again, have "put the pieces together." We can only surmise from the transcript of the appellate court that the circumstances did not rise to that level. So, once again, we seem to have a consistent theme, that the threat must be clear, unambiguous, and communicated to the therapist; none of these elements were present in this case.

Thompson v. Alameda County (1979)

This case involved a juvenile in a detention facility who stated that when he got out, he was going to "kill a child." He in fact was released and did sexually molest and kill a child. The family sued the county department of juvenile justice. The issue was whether a threat to kill "a child" was specific enough to trigger a duty to warn or a duty to protect. Warning could not be given since there was no specific victim; protecting a third party, namely a child in the Bay area, could not be carried out; there simply was no way to protect all of the children in a particular area. Apparently, the verbal statement of an intent to kill a child was insufficient as well to trigger involuntary commitment proceedings, so, despite the threat, the court found that there was no way protective action could be taken since the threat was so vague. We do not know whether staff members in the detention center attempted to pursue whether there was a third party that the young man had in mind and why they did not seek involuntary commitment. It may have been that the young man was not regarded as mentally ill and therefore could not be committed just based on a vague threat.

What we learn from this case is that there must be a "readily identifiable third party" in order for the duty to come into play. In this case, there was also an assertion of sovereign immunity, since it was a county agency being sued. Ultimately, the court found that while the violence was tragic, it was not something that could have been prevented. We cannot, once again, be held responsible for acts which we cannot control, although the concept of a "special relationship" is relevant; could the juvenile authorities have further detained the young man given his threats?

Hedlund v. the Superior Court of Orange County (1983)

This case involved the extension of the Duty to Protect third parties to those who are "reasonably foreseeable bystanders." This has its roots in tort law, which extends liability to people who are in the so-called "zone of danger." The prior case law did not deal with Duty to Protect but rather whether or not there was liability to a party who would be expected to be in close proximity with an intended victim.

In the case of *Hedlund*, an individual had been in psychotherapy, apparently court-ordered, and during the course of psychotherapy had made a comment to his therapist that the intended to kill his girlfriend, a woman by the name of Lanita Wilson. It appeared that the therapist took no protective action regarding Ms. Wilson. The patient in this case did, in fact, run Ms. Wilson's car off of the side of the road and proceeded to shoot into the car. In the car was not only Ms. Wilson, but also her three-year-old son. Ms. Wilson survived the shooting and filed a law suit against the Superior Court of Orange County. The suit sought damages not only for Ms. Wilson, but also for the psychological trauma to her son, who saw the shooting. The opposition to this, of course, came from individuals who stated that the son was not a direct victim.

The California Supreme Court, in its majority opinion, ruled that liability could indeed extend to anyone who would reasonably be in close proximity to an intended victim. The court further stated that it was reasonable to conclude that a three-year-old child might well be in close proximity to an intended victim and upheld that cause of action. During the appellate review, the American Psychological Association (APA) entered a very compelling *amicus curiae brief* that noted the vagueness of the statement, "reasonably expected to be in close proximity," and stated that it was so vague as to be totally unenforceable. The APA cited, for instance, the situation in which the intended victim was a schoolteacher—Would the potential liability then extend to all children in the school, since they might reasonably be in close proximity to the intended victim? Unfortunately, the APA brief was filed too late for the court to review it.

Nevertheless, there was a very compelling dissent from Justice Mosk of the California Supreme Court, who noted that the majority opinion unfortunately perpetuated the myth that mental health professionals have some sort of clairvoyant power to predict the future. Justice Mosk went on to criticize the majority, noting that there was no credible psychological or psychiatric literature that supported this noting and, in fact, most such literature pointed out that there was no such ability among mental health professional to accurately predict future violence. In review of many cases subsequent to *Hedlund*, it does not appear that this line of reasoning has been extended very far.

Brady v. Hopper (1983)

This case involved Dr. John Hopper, the psychiatrist in Denver, Colorado, who had had John Hinckley in treatment prior to Hinckley's attempted assassination of President Ronald Reagan in 1981. James Brady was President Reagan's press secretary and was seriously wounded in John Hinckley's shooting spree. The lawsuit alleged that Dr. Hopper knew or should have known of Hinckley's violent tendencies and that he should have taken protective action toward the intended victims. The case was summarily dismissed at the trial court level and Brady appealed it to the 10th Circuit Court of Appeals. Here, a detailed analysis of the case essentially supported the trial court but also rendered an opinion highly supportive of mental health professionals.

Apparently, Dr. Hopper had kept very meticulously detailed notes and it became very clear from those notes that John Hinckley had never said anything to him about his intentions to harm the President of the United States. He had not shared anything about his delusions regarding Jodie Foster, nor his delusions about his identifying with the main character in the movie, Taxi Driver. The 10th Circuit Court of Appeals issued an opinion, as noted above, supportive of the trial court, but made statements that greatly restrict the potential liability of mental health professionals. The court observed that even if Dr. Hopper had known about Hinckley's preoccupation with Jodie Foster, even if Dr. Hopper had known about his preoccupation with the movie, Taxi Driver, and even if Dr. Hopper had known that Hinckley took target practice at pictures of Ronald Reagan, all of those factors put together would still not constitute a foreseeable threat. In other words, there would have to be a direct communication of Mr. Hinckley to Dr. Hopper indicating that he intended to shoot or kill President Reagan before any Duty to Protect Third Parties could emerge.

Essentially, what the 10th Circuit Court of Appeals was stating here is that the procedure which we have discussed in earlier cases of hindsight bias or Monday morning quarterbacking should not apply. Clearly, after the fact, someone might be able to put together the fact that taking target practice at a picture of Ronald Reagan, along with delusions about the movie, Taxi Driver, and about Jodie Foster might indicate that Hinckley was planning to do something to harm Ronald Reagan in order to gain the attention and respect and undying love of Jodie Foster (since this was the essentially the theme in the movie, Taxi Driver). The court explicitly opined that such hindsight bias should not be used as a basis for professional liability.

As noted above, this is a decision that is very supportive of mental health professionals, for it underlies the need to do a comprehensive assessment when a threatening statement is being made but removes liability in cases where there is no such statement made, and that there is no need to do such an assessment if such a threatening statement is not made.

Davis v. Lhim (1983)

This case involved a psychiatric patient in the State of Michigan (Northville State Hospital), a man named John Patterson, who was admitted to the emergency room at Northville in a very agitated, apparently drug-induced psychotic state. While he was pacing in an agitated manner around the emergency room, a secretary in the emergency room overheard Mr. Patterson stating something to the effect that when his mother does not give him enough money to buy drugs, he feels like killing her. The statement was noted in Mr. Patterson's chart. Mr. Patterson was admitted for psychiatric treatment and remained in the psychiatric unit for approximately three months, under the care of Dr. Yong-Oh Lhim, a physician specializing in psychiatry. Apparently, once the drug was out of Mr. Patterson's system, he became very appropriate, was a model patient, and showed absolutely no signs of potential violence. He was, in fact, visited on several occasions by his mother and again the interactions were completely appropriate, demonstrating no verbal or physical aggression. He was discharged after three months and was in the custody of his aunt, Ms. Ruby Davis, and eventually went back to the State of Alabama to live with his mother.

Approximately 14 months after discharge, Mr. Patterson started to deteriorate psychologically. His mother came home from work one day and found her son holding a shotgun, apparently trying to ward off the terrorizing auditory hallucinations he was experiencing. The woman, unfortunately, tried to disarm her son and the gun went off, killing her. Ms. Davis then filed suit against Dr. Lhim and the state of Michigan and the plaintiff's lawyer obtained the services of a psychiatrist who testified that that one isolated statement in the emergency room should have been fair warning to the staff that this individual would be potentially violent toward his mother. Of course, this is a somewhat ludicrous statement on the part of the psychiatrist, since it was clearly the product of a drug-induced psychosis and all of the subsequent behavior was quite appropriate. Remarkably, the jury found for the plaintiff, holding Dr. Lhim and the state of Michigan liable, although the case was eventually reversed on appeal. However, once again from the point of risk assessment, we can analyze what went wrong here.

Apparently, a review of the psychiatric record revealed nothing in the discharge note regarding Mr. Patterson's previous statement of violence. One can speculate that the reason for this was that Dr. Lhim and his staff had seen only appropriate behavior and did not feel that it was important enough to include in a discharge note. This apparently came across to the jury, especially in light of the plaintiff's expert testimony, as some form of negligence. This highlights the point for us, in terms of risk assessment, that all aspects of potential violence, including threats that were never carried out, need to be accounted for in a discharge summary. In other words, had Dr. Lhim noted in the discharge note something to the effect that, "While Mr. Patterson had made threatening statements in the emergency room, his subsequent behavior which was completely appropriate, even including visits with his mother, indicates that the statements in the emergency room were purely the effects of drug intoxication and did not reflect any genuine attempt to harm his mother," the outcome might have been quite different. Unfortunately, there was no such statement in the chart and the jury saw it as negligence on the part of Dr. Lhim and his staff to have failed to factor that in.

Peck v. Counseling Service of Addison County (1985)

This case was unusual, in that the violence involved had to do with property damage. John Peck was a young man, apparently intellectually disabled and brain damaged, who was in treatment with a licensed mental health counselor at the Addison County Counseling Service in Addison County, Vermont. Apparently, Mr. Peck had made a statement to his therapist, the mental health counselor, that he was very angry with his father and he wanted to burn down his father's barn. The counselor was quite concerned about this and spent time above and beyond Mr. Peck's usual counseling session to obtain from him a "do no harm" agreement that he would not try to act out and burn down his father's barn. However, Mr. Peck did leave the counseling session and did do precisely that, burned down his father's barn. A lawsuit was then filed against the Counseling Service of Addison Country for failure to take reasonable steps to protect, in this case, the barn against the property damage.

While some people speculate that the point of the case was that there may have been people in the barn and therefore it was a Duty to Protect case, it really does have to do with the adequacy of the risk assessment, bringing it back to what we have been discussing all along. Mr. Peck was, of course, mentally retarded and had some degree of brain impairment. The mental health counselor was not trained in either of these areas and did not ask for a consultation with either a neurologist, who might evaluate the potential for violence of someone with this kind of brain impairment, nor a psychologist to do an intellectual evaluation and personality evaluation to determine the likelihood of acting out or the likelihood of understanding the "do no harm agreement." While we cannot perhaps fault the mental health counselor, who, in good faith, did what she was trained to do, there clearly was not a comprehensive assessment of Mr. Peck's potential for violent behavior, which would, of course, need to include these kinds of consultative efforts. Essentially, the mental health counselor, while acting in good faith, was practicing out of the bounds of his/her competence.

White v. United States (1986)

This case involved a patient named Dwayne White, who was a patient at the Forensic Services Division of Saint Elizabeth's Hospital in Washington, D.C., having been found Not Guilty by Reason of Insanity in 1968 for having killed a police officer. Mr. White progressed through the treatment program at the Forensic Programs Division, moving from a maximum security ward to a minimum security ward, and eventually having grounds privileges. While he was out on the ground, Mr. White met a female patient, who was in the Civil (rather than Forensic) Division. Mr. White and this woman fell in love and Mr. White asked for permission to marry this woman. The staff concluded that this would be therapeutic for Mr. White and allowed the hospital chaplain to marry them.

Shortly thereafter, his wife received a convalescent leave and moved off the hospital grounds, obtaining an apartment in the general area of the hospital. The hospital had no locked gates around it and Mr. White would go off the grounds to visit his wife. This was apparently well known to the staff, even though this was a technical violation of his grounds privileges. He was supposed to stay on the hospital grounds. However, Mr. White demonstrated completely appropriate behavior, was not reported for any violent behavior or any other kinds of infractions, and would always sign himself back into the hospital at the appropriate time. He also attended psychotherapy on a regular basis and participated fully in the treatment programs. Therefore, the staff essentially adopted an attitude of "benign indifference," figuring that his visits with his wife would be therapeutic, even though he was technically violating the conditions of his grounds privilege. On one occasion, Mr. White, while visiting his wife, was shown by his wife a picture of her in the company of another man, apparently at some sort of picnic. Mr. White flew into a rage, grabbed the closest thing to him which happened to be a pair of scissors, and stabbed his wife multiple times. Apparently, these were superficial wounds, none of them piercing any vital organs, and Ms. Genoa-White survived the attack. She then filed suit against Saint Elizabeth's Hospital (since it was a Federal hospital at that time, the lawsuit was against the United States).

The lawsuit alleged two separate theories of liability. The first was that the hospital violated its own grounds privileges status by allowing Mr. White to go off the grounds. The second involved the psychotherapy notes. Mr. White was in treatment with a senior member of the staff of the psychology service. Apparently, Mr. White had confided in that staff member that he was having violent fantasies about his wife.

The psychologist took these seriously and did an appropriate assessment, exploring the fantasies in-depth during the course of psychotherapy, asking for updated psychological testing, and consulting with various staff members about their perceptions of the seriousness or lack of seriousness of these fantasies. Based on all of the data, the therapist concluded that these were merely fantasies that could be dealt with in the course of psychotherapy, rather than any actual intention to do bodily harm.

In the legal proceedings, the trial court granted a summary judgment to the defendants, citing a theory of contributory negligence. This essentially meant that Mrs. Genoa-White "contributed" to the unfortunate outcome by freely inviting her husband to come to her apartment. Mrs. Genoa-White then appealed the case and it went to the United States Court of Appeals for the District of Columbia. In the appellate division, the court ruled that the hospital was negligent for failing to enforce its own standards regarding grounds privileges. However, from the point of view of risk assessment and professional liability of the psychologist involved, it said that the psychologist was not negligent for her actions, namely doing an in-depth analysis of the fantasies, ordering updated psychological testing, and consulting with other staff members, was an appropriate exercise of professional discretion, meeting the standard of care. Once again, this is a decision highly supportive of mental health professionals, in that it states that if the proper comprehensive assessment is done, we should not be found liable, regardless of the outcome.

Currie v. United States (1986)

This case involved a Vietnam veteran suffering from Post-Traumatic Stress Disorder. He was being seen for psychotherapy in a Veterans Administration (VA) Hospital in Durham, North Carolina. He had apparently lost his job at his place of employment, which was IBM, and he became quite agitated and started sharing fantasies with his therapist about killing people at IBM. The therapist in this situation took the threats very seriously and apparently "did everything right." In other words, he fully evaluated the veteran, concluded that the fantasies were, in fact, genuine threats, and consulted colleagues, including legal representatives at the hospital, as to whether this individual would satisfy the criteria for involuntary commitment. Apparently, the opinion of the hospital staff and of the legal staff was that he did not fulfill the criteria for involuntary commitment under North Carolina law, in that someone with a diagnosis of PTSD was not committable. Therefore, the therapist told his patient that he would not be able to commit him but that because of his credible threats, the therapist would remain in contact with IBM and would notify them when necessary.

The veteran apparently continued to be threatening and the therapist continued to keep the IBM staff apprised of threats. Apparently, during one session, the veteran had stated something to the effect that "You will read about me in tomorrow's papers." The therapist again notified the IBM staff, but somehow the veteran was able to get in with a loaded shotgun and killed several people. One of the survivors' families then filed suit, indicating that the VA Hospital was negligent. The court ruled, in a very fascinating finding, that while the hospital was wrong in failing to pursue involuntary commitment (the court believed that PTSD could be the basis for involuntary commitment), that, nevertheless, the hospital acted "in good faith," seeking out consultation and working out an intervention plan that satisfied the standard of care. Therefore, the court ruled, largely on the basis of the hospital's good faith attempt to follow appropriate standards, that the hospital was not negligent.

From the point of view of risk assessment, once again, it involves the careful integration of a large number of data sources, including consultation with other professionals and, in this case, even legal consultants.

Nasser v. Parker (1995)

This case involved the admission on a voluntary basis of a patient who had put a gun to the head of his girlfriend. The family of the girlfriend had convinced him that he needed to seek some treatment. He did so voluntarily and following the three days that the hospital could hold him, he appeared, in the opinion of the staff, to have made significant progress, to have become less agitated, and to have developed some degree of insight into his own behavior. He left the hospital without authorization and the hospital did not pursue any involuntary commitment. Eleven days later the patient did act out and killed his girlfriend and the girlfriend's family sued the hospital for professional negligence and Duty to Protect Third Parties. The court, interestingly enough, ruled in favor of the defendant, stating that a voluntary commitment involved an insufficient degree of control over the patient in order to justify the establishment of a special relationship. Recall that earlier in the understanding of the *Tarasoff* case, we had spoken about the "special relationship" and how it applied to psychotherapy, that it involved the theory that the professionals involved had the ability to control the behavior of the patient, while Ms. Tarasoff's brother, who roomed with Poddar, did not have such an ability. Unless there is an establishment of such a "special relationship," there can be no liability. In this case, the court essentially ruled that since a patient can sign himself out voluntarily after seventy-two hours, there was not enough control over the individual to justify calling it a "special relationship." Without a "special relationship," then there could be no obligation to protect third parties.

Sage v. US (1997)

This case was not terribly involved but did take the reasoning noted in *Nasser v. Parker* to another setting, namely outpatient psychotherapy. In this case, the patient was an outpatient and it was ruled that there is insufficient control of the therapist over an outpatient's behavior for it to be considered a "special relationship." This is a very important finding, for it harkens back to our original concerns in the *Tarasoff* case of how the concept of a "special relationship" could, in fact, be extended to outpatient psychotherapy.

Jablonski v. US (1983)

Mr. Jablonski was a man who was living with his wife, his stepdaughter, and his mother-in-law. Apparently, Mr. Jablonski had an extensive history of domestic violence with previous partners. Mr. Jablonski had apparently assaulted his mother-in-law and his wife attempted to get him hospitalized at the local Veterans Administration (VA) Hospital, since Mr. Jablonski was a veteran. Starting at the emergency room, there were a series of human errors. The police, in conveying Mr. Jablonski to the emergency room, had noted or had passed on to the doctors there that they should be concerned about Mr. Jablonski since he had been violent in the past. Apparently, this was not documented and was not conveyed to the psychiatrist who eventually examined Mr. Jablonski. There were apparently hospital records at the VA hospital and at others which could have been obtained but which were not. When the psychiatrist examined Mr. Jablonski, he was not aware of the police warnings and was not aware of Mr. Jablonski's prior history, nor prior hospitalizations, nor apparently did he attempt to obtain any of the prior records. He decided that Mr. Jablonski could be seen as an outpatient and did not recommend inpatient hospitalization.

Mr. Jablonski soon thereafter killed his wife. A lawsuit was brought against the VA hospital (hence Jablonski v. United States) on behalf of the minor child, named Megan. The interesting issue here was that the family was well aware of the fact that Mr. Jablonski had assaulted someone. However, unlike cases before, there was no direct threat by Mr. Jablonski to an intended victim. Recall that he had not threatened his wife and, in fact, his assaultive behavior in the past had been directed against his mother-in-law. Nevertheless, the court ruled that the VA hospital should be held liable because his wife fit the "psychological profile" of prior victims. While this would certainly be an appropriate ruling in domestic violence situations which do, indeed, repeat themselves quite frequently, it becomes somewhat problematic when one tries to extend the concept of "psychological profile" of an intended victim too broadly. We have discussed before the phenomenon of "hindsight bias," or what is often referred to as "Monday morning quarterbacking." After the fact, one can always see aspects of the victim which fit the "profile," however loosely defined, of previous victims. In other words, a plaintiff's expert witness could argue that this individual met the "profile" because they have the same color hair, the same color eyes, were overweight, were underweight, or were African-American/Caucasian/etc. The court was not very precise in referring to the concept of "psychological profile."

While this is an unfortunate choice of words and can lead to a great deal of mischief in terms of legal liability, there were several aspects of the Jablonski case that were quite important in terms of risk assessment. The fact that no attention was paid to the police warnings, no attempt made to review prior records, and no attempt on the part of the psychiatrist who interviewed Mr. Jablonski to obtain an accurate prior history are all important aspects of a comprehensive risk assessment. Therefore, from the point of view that we have been describing, of the elements that must go into a comprehensive risk assessment, the case of Jablonski falls far short.

Lipari v. Sears, Roebuck (1980)

This case involved a chronically ill schizophrenic individual by the name of Ulysses Cribbs, who was in treatment at the outpatient Veterans Administration (VA) hospital in Omaha, Nebraska. Mr. Cribbs had had a history of de-compensating and becoming violent when he did so, usually precipitated by his failure to take his medication. The therapist at the outpatient clinic observed that Mr. Cribbs was deteriorating and asked him to enter the VA hospital for inpatient treatment. Mr. Cribbs became very agitated, refused to sign himself in, and went storming out of the therapy session. He then went to a local Sears, Roebuck Store, purchased a shotgun and not too long thereafter went to a crowded nightclub in Omaha, Nebraska, and started firing at random people in the dining room of the nightclub. He killed a man named Dennis Lipari and seriously wounded his wife. When Mrs. Lipari recovered, she filed suit against Sears, Roebuck, who sold him the shotgun, and they sued the VA hospital for letting a psychotic patient be in a position where he could, in fact, purchase a shotgun.

The case against Sears, Roebuck was eventually granted a summary judgment and it went on to be a case of liability against the VA hospital. The plaintiffs had two causes of action, one of which was a Duty to Protect Third Parties, which was quickly dismissed because in this case there was no identifiable third party, nor were there any threats to specific individuals. However, the court did find the hospital negligent for failure to initiate involuntary commitment proceedings. That is, it was seen as a failure to exercise reasonable judgment in terms of a therapeutic intervention. Rather than trying to involuntarily commit Mr. Cribbs at the time that he was de-compensating, the hospital merely signed his discharge "Against Medical Advice." The court noted that his past history of violent behavior associated with periods of time when he was psychotic would have been sufficient to justify involuntary commitment.

What this case illustrates, from the view of risk assessment, is that we cannot be too narrow in conducting these assessments, thinking that they deal only with a Duty to Protect Third Parties. We have to evaluate the threat in general and see what would be the most appropriate kind of intervention. In this case, the court ruled that the appropriate intervention would have been involuntary commitment.

Williamson v. Liptzin (2000)

This case involved a student, apparently in law school, who was seeing a psychiatrist at the student health service at a university. The psychiatrist whom he was seeing announced to him that he was retiring in several months and that the student should try to follow up treatment "with someone with my same approach," indicating that he thought that the student was doing well and was benefiting from the kind of medication that the psychiatrist was prescribing. However, the psychiatrist did not make any specific referrals nor give the student a list of names. Following that, the student apparently went home for vacation, did not pursue treatment, and by the time he returned to school was quite psychotic and once again did not follow through with treatment. He eventually went into a downtown area, clad in Army fatigues, and shot and killed a number of people.

The family of one of the survivors of the shooting filed suit against Dr. Liptzin, alleging, among other matters, a Duty to Protect Third Parties. Once again, of course, since there was no identifiable victim, there was no Duty to Protect. However, the jury did find for the plaintiff because they regarded the Doctor's lack of seeking out a list of referral sources as "cavalier." From the point of view of risk assessment, we must arrange for careful follow-up, if we are concerned about a client's future behavior. Here, the psychiatrist was clearly concerned for he felt the young man needed further treatment, but essentially was found liable for failure to follow through on those concerns. What is the lesson to be derived from this case? Clearly, if our risk assessment raises any concerns, we need to follow through with a plan of treatment or intervention, or at the very least, make a bonafide effort to refer the client or patient.

Ewing v. Goldstein (2004)

This case, from the state of California, is one of the most recent which extends the concept of who is a patient to a family member. In this case, a therapist had been treating a young man who was romantically involved with a woman. While he had made statements regarding his frustration about the relationship with the woman he had never confided in the therapist any intent to harm the woman. On one occasion, the therapist received from the patient's father a phone call indicating that the son had communicated to him a threat to kill the girlfriend. The therapist was, of course, concerned, and tried to have the patient hospitalized. The hospital refused to accept him as an involuntary commitment, and he eventually did kill his girlfriend.

The interesting point at issue here was whether the family member who communicated the concern could be regarded as part and parcel of the patient, or did it actually have to be the patient who communicated the threat to the therapist. The court ruled that the family could in fact be regarded as an extension of the patient in this situation, and that the therapist did have a Duty to Protect the Third Party who was endangered. What is of some interest here, was whether or not there was liability against the hospital that refused to commit him.

Chapter 4
Conclusions

In this brief volume, we have looked at the field of risk assessment from a number of different perspectives, including its historical roots, legal statutes, and court cases that have arisen from the practice, psychological risk factors and myths, frequently used risk assessment instruments, and, perhaps most importantly, implications for treatment providers.

We have noted that the courts were initially unresponsive to the concerns of mental health professionals who tried to discuss the limitations of such assessments, though currently, some cases have emerged that reflect a growing sensitivity on the part of court to psychological research and to proper standards for risk assessments. We have also reviewed the developments and controversies in the field of risk assessment.

Indeed, researchers have sometimes talked about the three generations of risk assessment, with the purely clinical approach regarded as the first generation, the purely actuarial approach identified as the second, and structured professional judgment labeled as the third. Ultimately, our contention is that it is now time for a new generation, one in which actuarial assessment and structured professional judgment pool their resources rather than argue over which is best. Moreover, there must be a recognition of the subtleties and nuances inherent in any such assessment, as they reveal, truly, that *one size does not fit all.*

D.L. Shapiro and A.M. Noe, *Risk Assessment*,
SpringerBriefs in Behavioral Criminology, DOI 10.1007/978-3-319-17058-9_4

References

American Psychiatric Association. (2000). *Diagnostic and statistical manual of mental disorders* (4th ed., text revision). Washington, DC: Author.

American Psychiatric Association. (2013). *Diagnostic and statistical manual of mental disorders* (5th ed.). Arlington, VA: Author.

Arbisi, P. (2003). Review of the HCR-20: Assessing risk for violence. In B. S. Plake, J. C. Impara, & R.A. Spies (Eds.), *The fifteenth mental measurements yearbook.* Retrieved from the Burros Institute's Mental Measurements Yearbook online database.

Austin, J., Peyton, J., & Johnson, K. D. (2003). *Reliability and validity study of the static-99/ RRASOR sex offender risk assessment instruments: Final report submitted to the Pennsylvania Board of Probation and Parole.* Washington, DC: The Institute on Crime, Justice and Corrections at George Washington University.

Barbaree, H., Langton, C., Blanchard, R., & Boer, D. (2008). Predicting recidivism in sex offenders using the SVR-20: The contribution of age-at-release. *International Journal of Forensic Mental Health, 7*, 47–64.

Baxstrom v. Herold, 383 US 107 (1966).

Barefoot v. Estelle, 463 US 880 (1983)

Becker, J., Doran, D., & Matson, S. (2014, May). *Intervention strategies for violent offenders.* Session presented at the American Psychological Association—American Bar Association National Conference on Violence, Washington, D.C.

Boer, D., Hart, S., Kropp, R., & Webster, C. (1997). *Manual for the sexual violence risk-20.* Burnaby, BC, Canada: Mental Health, Law, and Policy Institute at Simon Fraser University.

Borum, R. (2007). Improving the clinical practice of violence risk assessment: Technology, guidelines, and training. In H. Bloom & C. D. Webster (Eds.), *Essential writings in violence risk assessment and management* (pp. 53–75). Toronto, ON, Canada: Centre for Addiction and Mental Health.

Bourgon, G. (2011). Assessing the risk of domestic violence offenders. *Public Safety Canada, Research Summary, 16* (3). Retrieved from: http://www.publicsafety.gc.ca/cnt/rsrcs/%20 pblctns/dmstc-ffndrs/dmstc-ffndrs-eng.pdf

Bowen, E. (2011). An overview of partner violence risk assessment and the potential role of female victim risk appraisals. *Aggression and Violent Behavior, 16*, 214–226.

Boyle, D., O'Leary, K., Rosenbaum, A., & Hassett-Walker, C. (2008). Differentiating between generally and partner-only violent subgroups: Lifetime antisocial behavior, family of origin violence, and impulsivity. *Journal of Family Violence, 23*(1), 47–55.

Brady v. Hopper, 570 F. Supp. 1333 (D. Colo., 1983).

D.L. Shapiro and A.M. Noe, *Risk Assessment*,
SpringerBriefs in Behavioral Criminology, DOI 10.1007/978-3-319-17058-9

Budrionis, R. (2003). Review of the sexual violence risk-20. In B. S. Plake, J. C. Impara, & R.A. Spies (Eds.), *The fifteenth mental measurements yearbook*. Retrieved from the Burros Institute's Mental Measurements Yearbook online database.

Campbell, T. (2007). *Assessing sex offenders: Problems and pitfalls*. Springfield, IL: Thomas Books.

Cawood, J., & Corcoran, M. (2009). *Violence assessment and intervention: The practitioner's handbook* (2nd ed.). Boca Raton, Fl: CRC Press.

Cleckley, H. (1976). *The mask of sanity: An attempt to clarify some issues about the so-called psychopathic personality* (5th ed.). St. Louis, MO: Mosby.

Cocozza, J., & Steadman, H. (1976). The failure of psychiatric predictions of dangerousness: Clear and convincing evidence. *Rutgers Law Review, 29*, 1084–1101.

Conroy, M., & Murrie, D. (2007). *Forensic assessment of violence risk: A guide for risk assessment and risk management*. Hoboken, NJ: Wiley.

Currie v. United States, 644 F.Supp. 1074 (M.D.N.C., 1986).

Davis v. Lhim, 124 Mich.App. 291, 335 N.W.2d 481 (Mich. App., 1983).

DeClue, G. (2002). Avoiding garbage in sex offender re-offense risk assessment: A case study. *Journal of Threat Assessment, 2*, 73–92.

Douglas, K., Shaffer, C., Blanchard, A., Guy, L., Reeves, K., & Weir, J. (2014). *HCR-20 violence risk assessment scheme: Overview and annotated bibliography*. Burnaby, BC, Canada: Mental Health, Law, and Policy Institute at Simon Fraser University.

Dvoskin, J., & Dlugacz, H. (2014, May). *Violent offender re-entry into society*. Session presented at the American Psychological Association—American Bar Association National Conference on Violence, Washington, D.C.

Epperson, D., Kaul, J., Huot, S., Goldman, R., & Alexander, W. (2003). *Minnesota sex offender screening tool-revised (MnSOST-R) technical paper: Development, validation, and recommended risk level cut scores*. St. Paul, MN: Minnesota Department of Corrections.

Epperson, D., Kaul, J., Huot, S., Hesselton, D., & Alexander, W. (2005). *Minnesota sex offender screening tool-revised (MnSOST-R) instructions*. St. Paul, MN: Minnesota Department of Corrections.

Estelle v. Smith, 451 US 454 (1981).

Ewing v. Goldstein, 120 Cal. App. 4th 807, 15 Cal.Rptr. 3d 864 (Cal. App., 2004).

Firestone, P., Bradford, J. M., Greenberg, D. M., & Serran, G. A. (2000). The relationship between deviant sexual arousal and psychopathy in incest offenders, extrafamilial child molesters, and rapists. *Journal of the American Academy of Psychiatry and the Law, 28*, 303–308.

Forth, A., Kosson, D., & Hare, R. (2003). *The hare PCL: Youth version*. Toronto, ON: Multi-Health Systems.

Fulero, S. (1995). Review of the hare psychopathy checklist-revised. In J. C. Conoley & J. C. Impara (Eds.), *The twelfth mental measurements yearbook*. Retrieved from the Burros Institute's Mental Measurements Yearbook online database.

Gabbard, G. (2005). *Psychodynamic psychiatry in clinical practice*. Arlington, VA: American Psychiatric Publishing Inc.

Hanson, R. (1997). *The development of a brief actuarial risk scale for sex offense recidivism*. (User Report 1997-04). Ottawa, ON, Canada: Department of the Solicitor General of Canada.

Hanson, R. (2001). *Age and sexual recidivism: A comparison of rapists and child molesters* (User Report 2001-01). Ottawa, ON, Canada: Department of the Solicitor General of Canada

Hanson, R., & Bussiere, M. (1996). *Predictors of sexual offender recidivism: A meta- analysis* (User Report 96-04). Ottawa, ON, Canada: Department of the Solicitor General of Canada.

Hanson, R., & Bussiere, M. (1998). Predicting relapse: A meta-analysis of sexual offender recidivism studies. *Journal of Consulting and Clinical Psychology, 66*, 348–362.

Hanson, R., Lloyd, C., Helmus, L., & Thornton, D. (2012). Developing non-arbitrary metrics for risk communication: Percentile ranks for the static-99/r and static-2002/r sexual offender risk tools. *International Journal of Forensic Mental Health, 11*(1), 9–23.

Hanson, R., & Morton-Bourgon, K. (2005). The characteristics of persistent sexual offenders: A meta-analysis of recidivism studies. *Journal of Consulting and Clinical Psychology, 73*(6), 1154–1163.

Hanson, R., & Morton-Bourgon, K. (2007). *The accuracy of recidivism risk assessments for sexual offenders: A meta-analysis.* Corrections User Report No. 2007-01. Ottawa, ON, Canada: Public Safety and Emergency Preparedness Canada.

Hanson, R., & Morton-Bourgon, K. (2009). The accuracy of recidivism risk assessments for sexual offenders: A meta-analysis of 118 prediction studies. *Psychological Assessment, 21*(1), 1–21.

Hanson, R., & Thornton, D. (1999). *Static-99: Improving actuarial risk assessments for sex offenders.* User Report 99-02. Ottawa, ON, Canada: Department of the Solicitor General of Canada.

Hanson, R., & Thornton, D. (2003). *Notes on the development of the static- 2002.* User Report No. 2003-01. Ottawa, ON, Canada: Department of the Solicitor General of Canada.

Hare, R. (1980). A research scale for the assessment of psychopathy in criminal populations. *Personality and Individual differences, 3*, 35–42.

Hare, R. (1991). *Manual for the hare psychopathy checklist-revised.* Toronto, ON, Canada: Multi-Health Systems.

Hare, R. (1996). Psychopathy and antisocial personality disorder: A case of diagnostic confusion. *Psychiatric Times, 13*(2), 39–40.

Hare, R. (1998). The hare PCL-R: Some issues concerning its use and misuse. *Legal and Criminological Psychology, 3*, 99–119.

Hare, R. (2003). *Manual for the revised psychopathy checklist* (2nd ed.). Toronto, ON, Canada: Multi-Health Systems.

Hare, R., Hart, S., & Harpur, T. (1991). Psychopathy and the DSM-IV criteria for antisocial personality disorder. *Journal of Abnormal Psychology, 100*(3), 391–398.

Harpur, T., Hare, R., & Hakstian, A. (1989). Two-factor conceptualization of psychopathy: Construct validity and assessment implications. *Psychological Assessment, 1*(1), 6–17.

Harris, G., Phenix, A., Hanson, R., & Thornton, D. (2003). *Static-99 coding rules: Revised 2003.* Ottawa, ON, Canada: Department of the Solicitor General of Canada.

Harris, G., Rice, M., & Quinsey, V. (1993). Violent recidivism of mentally disordered offenders: The development of a statistical prediction instrument. *Criminal Justice and Behavior, 20*(4), 315–335.

Harris, G., Rice, M., & Quinsey, V. (1994). Psychopathy as a taxon: Evidence that psychopaths are a discrete class. *Journal of Consulting and Clinical Psychology, 62*(2), 387–397.

Hart, S. (1998). The role of psychopathy in assessing risk for violence: Conceptual and methodological issues. *Legal and Criminological Psychology, 3*, 121–137.

Hart, S., Cox, D., & Hare, R. (1995). *The hare psychopathy checklist: Screening version.* Toronto, ON, Canada: Multi-Health Systems.

Hart, S., Kropp, P., & Hare, R. (1988). Performance of male psychopaths following conditional release from prison. *Journal of Consulting Psychology, 56*(2), 227–232.

Hedlund v. Superior Court, 34 Cal. 3d 695, 194 Cal.Rptr. 805, 669 P.2d 41 (Cal., 1983).

Heilbrun, K. (2009). *Evaluation for risk of violence in adults.* New York: Oxford University Press.

Helmus, L., & Bourgon, G. (2011). Taking stock of 15 years of research on the spousal assault risk assessment guide (SARA): A critical review. *International Journal of Forensic Mental Health, 10*, 64–75.

Helmus, L., Hanson, R., & Thornton, D. (2009). Reporting static-99 in light of new research on recidivism norms. *The Forum, 21* (1). *Winter, 2009*, 38–45.

Helmus, L., Thornton, D., Hanson, R., & Babchishin, K. (2011). *Assessing the risk of older sex offenders: Developing the static-99r and static-2002r.* Corrections Research User Report 2011-01. Ottawa, ON, Canada: Public Safety Canada.

Helmus, L., Thornton, D., Hanson, R., & Babchishin, K. (2012). Improving the predictive accuracy of static-99 and static-2002 with older sex offenders: Revised age weights. *Sexual Abuse: Journal of Research and Treatment, 24*(1), 64–101.

Hilton, N., & Harris, G. (2007). Assessing risk of intimate partner violence. In J. Campbell (Ed.), *Assessing dangerousness: Violence by batterers and child abusers* (pp. 105–125). New York: Springer Publishing Company LLC.

Hilton, N., Harris, G., & Rice, M. (2001). Predicting violence by serious wife assaulters. *Journal of Interpersonal Violence, 16*, 408–423.

Hilton, N., Harris, G., & Rice, M. (2010). *Risk assessment for domestically violent men*. Washington, DC: American Psychological Association.

Hilton, N., Harris, G., Rice, M., Houghton, R., & Eke, A. (2008). An in-depth actuarial risk assessment for wife assault recidivism: The domestic violence risk appraisal guide. *Law and Human Behavior, 32*, 150–163.

Hoberman, H. (2001). Dangerousness and sex offenders: Assessing risk for future sexual offenses. In A. Schlank (Ed.), *The sexual predator: Legal issues, clinical issues, special populations* (Vol. II). Kingston, NJ: Civic Research Institute.

Jablonski by Pahls v. US 712 F.2d 391 (C.A. 9 (Cal.), 1983).

Jurek v. Texas, 428 US 262 (1976).

Kansas v. Crane, 534 US 407, 122 S. Ct. 867, 151 L.Ed.2d 856 (U.S., 2002).

Katz, I. (2003). Review of the spousal assault risk assessment Guide. In B. S. Plake, J. C. Impara, & R.A. Spies (Eds.), *The fifteenth mental measurements yearbook*. Retrieved from the Burros Institute's Mental Measurements Yearbook online database.

Kropp, P., Hart, S., Webster, C., & Eaves, D. (1995). *Manual for the spousal assault risk assessment guide* (2nd ed.). Vancouver, BC, Canada: British Columbia Institute on Family Violence.

Kropp, P., Hart, S., Webster, C., & Eaves, D. (1999). *Spousal assault risk assessment guide (SARA)*. Toronto, ON, Canada: Multi-Health Systems.

Lessard v. Schmidt, 349 F. Supp. 1078 (E.D. Wis., 1972).

Lipari v. Sears, Roebuck & Co., 497 F. Supp. 185 (D. Neb., 1980).

Marcus, D., John, S., & Edens, J. (2004). A taxometric analysis of psychopathic personality. *Journal of Abnormal Psychology, 113*, 626–635.

McGrath, R., Cumming, G., Burchard, B., Zeoli, S., & Ellerby, L. (2010). *Current practices and emerging trends in sexual abuser management*. Brandon, VT: Safer Society Press.

McIntosh v. Milano, 168 N.J.Super. 466, 403 A.2d 500 (N.J.Super.L., 1979).

McNeil, D., Gregory, A., Lam, J., Binder, R., & Sullivan, G. (2003). Utility of decision support tools for assessing acute risk of violence. *Journal of Consulting and Clinical Psychology, 71*, 945–953.

Meehl, P. (1954). *Clinical versus statistical prediction: A theoretical analysis and a review of the evidence*. Minneapolis, MN: University of Minnesota Press.

Meloy, J. (2000). *Violence risk and threat assessment: A practical guide for mental health and criminal justice professionals*. San Diego, CA: Specialized Training Services.

Monahan, J. (1981). *Predicting violent behavior: An assessment of clinical techniques*. Beverly Hills, CA: Sage.

Monahan, J. (1992). Mental disorder and violent behavior: Perceptions and evidence. *American Psychologist, 47*(4), 511–521.

Monahan, J., Steadman, H., Silver, E., Appelbaum, P., Robbins, P., Mulvey, E., et al. (2001). *Rethinking risk assessment: The MacArthur study of mental disorder and violence*. New York: Oxford University Press.

Murrie, D., Boccaccini, M., Caperton, J., & Rufino, K. (2012). Field validity of the psychopathy checklist–revised in sex offender risk assessment. *Psychological Assessment, 24*(2), 524–529.

Nasser v. Parker, 249 Va. 172, 455 S.E.2d 502 (Va., 1995).

Novaco, R. (2003). *The Novaco Anger scale and Provocation Inventory (NAS-PI)*. Los Angeles, CA: Western Psychological Services.

Olmi, D. (2005). Review of the Hare Psychopathy Checklist-Revised: 2nd Edition. In R. A. Spies & B. S. Plake (Eds.), *The sixteenth mental measurements yearbook*. Retrieved from the Burros Institute's Mental Measurements Yearbook online database.

Peck v. Counseling Service of Addison County, Inc., 146 Vt. 61, 499 A.2d 422 (Vt., 1985).

Phenix, A., Doren, D., Helmus, L., Hanson, R., & Thornton, D. (2008). *Coding rules for static-2002*. Ottawa, ON, Canada: Public Safety Canada.

Quinsey, V., Harris, G., Rice, M., & Cormier, C. (1998). *Violent Offenders: Appraising and Managing Risk*. Washington, DC: American Psychological Association.

Quinsey, V., Harris, G., Rice, M., & Cormier, C. (2006). *Violent offenders: Appraising and managing risk* (2nd ed.). Washington, DC: American Psychological Association.

Quinsey, V., Rice, M., & Harris, G. (1995). Actuarial prediction of sexual recidivism. *Journal of Interpersonal Violence, 10*, 85–105.

Rogers, R., & Graves-Oliver, D. (2003). Psychological and psychiatric measures in forensic practice. In R. Rosner (Ed.), *Principles and practice of forensic psychology* (2nd ed., pp. 621–630). Boca Raton, Fl: CRC Press.

Sage v. U.S., 974 F.Supp. 851 (E.D. Va., 1997).

Shaw v. Glickman, 415 A.2d 625, 45 Md.App. 718 (Md. App., 1980).

Singh, J., Grann, M., & Fazel, S. (2013). Authorship bias in violence risk assessment? A systematic review and meta-Analysis. *PLoS ONE, 8*(9), e72484. doi:10.1371/journal.pone.0072484.

Steadman, H., & Cocozza, J. (1974). *Careers of the criminally insane: Excessive social control of deviance*. Lexington, MA: Lexington Books.

Szmukler, G. (2001). Violence risk prediction in practice. *British Journal of Psychiatry, 178*, 84–85.

Tarasoff v. Regents of University of California, 17 Cal.3d 425, 131 Cal.Rptr. 14 (Cal., 1976).

Thompson v. Alameda County, 152 Cal.Rptr. 226, 88 Cal.App.3d 936 (Cal.App. 1 Dist., 1979).

Thornberry, T., & Jacoby, J. (1979). *The criminally insane: A community follow-up of mentally ill offenders*. Chicago, IL: University of Chicago Press.

United States v. Salerno, 631 F.Supp. 1364 (S.D.N.Y., 1986).

U.S. Department of Homeland Security. (2008). *Active shooter: How to respond*. Washington, D.C.: Author.

U.S. Department of Justice. (2014). *Criminal Victimization, 2013* (NCJ 247648). Retrieved from http://www.bjs.gov/content/pub/pdf/cv13.pdf.

Varela, J., Boccaccini, M., Murrie, D., Caperton, J., & Gonzalez, E. (2013). Do the Static-99 and Static-99R perform similarly for white, black, and latino sexual offenders? *Journal of Forensic Mental Health, 12*, 231–243.

Webster, C., Douglas, K., Eaves, D., & Hart, S. (19e97). *HCR-20: Assessing risk for violence* (version 2). Vancouver, BC, Canada: Simon Fraser University.

Webster, C., Harris, G., Rice, M., Cormier, C., & Quinsey, V. (1994). *The violence prediction scheme: Assessing dangerousness in high risk men*. Toronto, ON, Canada: University of Toronto.

White v. U.S., 780 F.2d 97, 250 US App.D.C. 435 (C.A.D.C., 1986).

Williamson v. Liptzin, 141 N.C. App. 1, 539 S.E.2d 313 (N.C. App., 2000).

Yang, Y., Raine, A., Colletti, P., Toga, A., & Narr, K. (2009a). Abnormal temporal and prefrontal cortical gray matter thinning in psychopaths. *Molecular Psychiatry, 14*, 561–562.

Yang, Y., Raine, A., Narr, K., Colletti, P., & Toga, A. (2009b). Localization of deformations within the amygdala in individuals with psychopathy. *Archive of General Psychiatry, 66*, 986–994.

Young v. Weston, 898 F.Supp. 744 (W.D. Wash., 1995).

CPSIA information can be obtained at www.ICGtesting.com
Printed in the USA
LVOW07s1933270315

432329LV00002B/6/P

9 783319 170572